www.prim-ed.com

READING
COMPREHENSION AND WORD READING

GW00454880

Lesson Plans, Texts, Comprehension Activities, Word Reading Activities and Assessments for the Year 1 English Curriculum.

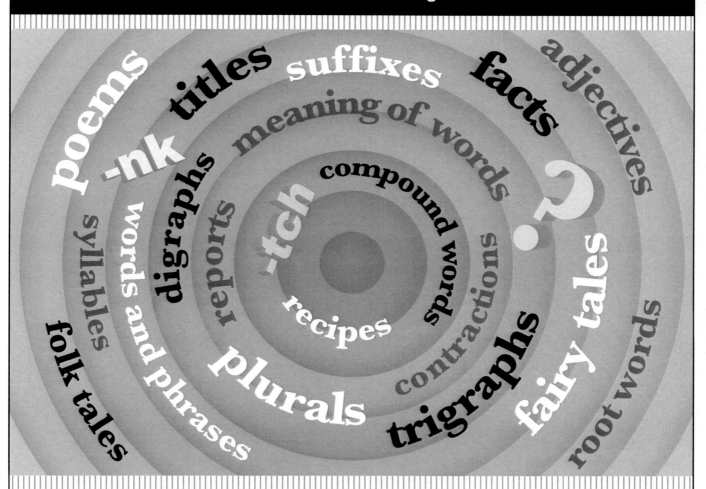

Monitor and track pupil progress with a FREE digital assessment tool.

COMPREHENSION

- ☑ Wide variety of text genres
- ☑ Activities to deepen comprehension
- ☑ Self-assessment for pupils

WORD READING

- ☑ Focus on word reading elements
- ☑ Activities to practise word reading skills
- ☑ Self-assessment for pupils

Reading – Comprehension and Word Reading (Year 1)

Published by Prim-Ed Publishing® 2015
Copyright© R.I.C. Publications® 2015

ISBN 978-1-84654-794-2

PR–2975

Titles available in this series:

Internet websites

In some cases, websites or specific URLs may be recommended. While these are checked and rechecked at the time of publication, the publisher has no control over any subsequent changes which may be made to webpages. It is *strongly* recommended that the class teacher checks *all* URLs before allowing pupils to access them.

View all pages online

Email address: sales@prim-ed.com   Home page: http://www.prim-ed.com

Foreword

• •

Reading – Comprehension and Word Reading is a six-book series written to support the teaching, learning and assessment of the programmes of study for reading at key stages one and two. The books give equal focus to the dimensions of comprehension and word reading, and the different kinds of teaching and learning experiences needed for each.

Titles in this series are:

- *Reading – Comprehension and Word Reading – Year 1*
- *Reading – Comprehension and Word Reading – Year 2*
- *Reading – Comprehension and Word Reading – Year 3*
- *Reading – Comprehension and Word Reading – Year 4*
- *Reading – Comprehension and Word Reading – Year 5*
- *Reading – Comprehension and Word Reading – Year 6*

Contents

Format of the Books

There are 18 six-page units of work within each book, and three formal summative assessment units, one located after every six units.

Each of the 18 units relates to a specific genre of fiction or non-fiction and follows the same format:

A table of **Curriculum Links** is provided, which lists the curriculum objectives covered by the text, comprehension and word reading pupil pages. An outcome is listed for each objective, to aid teacher assessment. Each objective has been allocated a code to aid identification. A table listing these codes and objectives can be found on page xi.

The **Definition of Terms** section includes an explanation of technical literary and grammatical terms. Generally, these terms are not covered in the glossary supplied with the programmes of study for English. They are provided as an aid for the teacher and not for pupils to learn, although teachers may wish to use the information to assist pupils to understand and complete specific activities.

Links to other Curriculum Areas lists any statutory or non-statutory content relating to other programmes of study. This section is omitted if no links are included.

Teacher Page 1

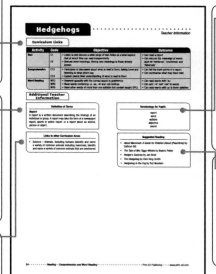

Terminology for Pupils is a list of technical literary and grammatical terms included in the unit. Pupils need to understand and use the terminology to complete the unit's activities.

Suggested Reading includes fiction and non-fiction books and/or digital material that relate to the content of the unit.

The **Notes and Guidance** provide detailed teaching points relating to each of the three pupil activity pages: text; comprehension; and word reading.

There are also assessment activities and answers.

Teacher Pages 2 and 3

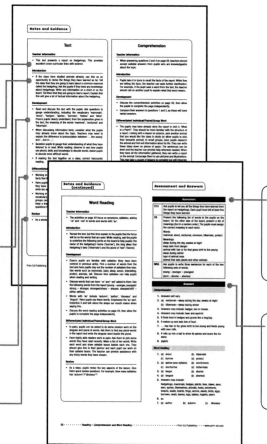

The **Teacher Information** states the content of the copymaster activity and/or any materials the pupils may need.

The **Introduction** provides an activity for the class to complete before commencing the copymaster activity. It might involve a discussion, retelling the text in sequence or rereading the text in search of something specific.

Activities listed in the **Development** section might introduce or revise topics and/or suggest items to discuss, all with the aim of aiding pupils to work on the copymaster activity pages independently.

The **Differentiated Individual/Paired/Group Work** suggests differentiated additional activities related to the pupil activity pages.

The **Review** provides opportunities to discuss and/or share work to assess and conclude each activity.

The **Assessment** table provides assessment activities for the pupil copymaster activity pages.

All the **Answers** are provided for the comprehension and word reading activity pages.

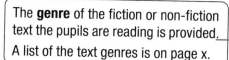

Format of the Books

Pupil Page 1

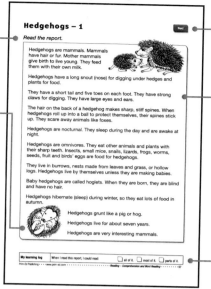

The **genre** of the fiction or non-fiction text the pupils are reading is provided. A list of the text genres is on page x.

The **artwork** illustrates and supports the text.

The **Text focus** of the page is indicated.

Where possible, the **vocabulary in the texts** includes words from the spelling work and the spelling word list outlined in English Appendix 1 for each key stage.

The **learning log** provides an opportunity for pupils to self-assess their reading of the text.

Pupil Page 2

Comprehension **questions and activities** relating to the text on *Pupil Page 1* are provided. The comprehension questions may relate to text structure or language features as well as text meaning.

The **learning log** provides an opportunity for pupils to self-assess their completion of the activities.

The **Comprehension focus** of the page is indicated.

The **answers** are provided on *Teacher Page 3.*

Pupil Page 3

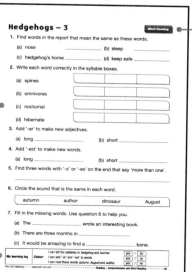

Word Reading questions and activities relating to the text on *Pupil Page 1* are provided. The main focus is the development of new vocabulary.

The **learning log** provides an opportunity for pupils to self-assess their completion of the activities.

The **Word Reading focus** of the page is indicated.

A list of the word reading concepts covered is on page x.

The **answers** are provided on *Teacher Page 3.*

There is a digital assessment tool to accompany each book in the *Reading – Comprehension and Word Reading* series. This will enable teachers to monitor and track pupil progress. Teachers can download this assessment tool from the *Prim-Ed Publishing* website (www.prim-ed.com).

The home page of the download has the following features:

- Instructions for teachers;
- Quick-glance curriculum objectives and codes;
- Assessment by curriculum objectives; and
- Assessment by units in *Reading – Comprehension and Word Reading*.

Clicking the **Instructions for the teacher** icon provides an overview of the features of the download.

Clicking the **Quick-glance curriculum objectives and codes** icon shows the comprehension and word reading objectives from the curriculum and the codes that have been assigned to them in the book.

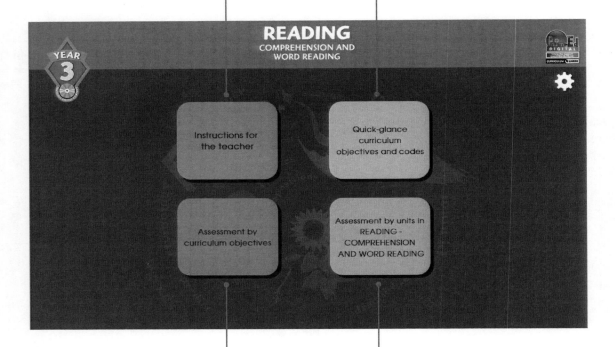

Clicking the **Assessment by curriculum objectives** icon displays each curriculum objective in a linear fashion, with advice and guidance to assess each one (more details are given on page vii).

Clicking the **Assessment by units in *Reading – Comprehension and Word Reading*** icon reveals an overview page allowing the teacher to click on the following options:

- Units (each individual unit in the book can be clicked);
- Formal Assessment (each of the three formal assessments can be clicked);
- Term (the three terms can be clicked); and
- End-of-Year (an overview of the pupil's yearly achievement).

Three categories and colour classifications of pupil progress are used throughout the assessment download. These categories are: working towards expectations (red), meeting expectations (orange) and exceeding expectations (green).

Teachers can assess by:

1. Curriculum objectives

- Click **Assessment by curriculum objectives** on the home page.

- Click on the code of the objective you are assessing. (Refer to the **Curriculum Objectives and Codes** on page xi, or click the quick-glance icon on the home page of the assessment tool and print them out.)

Type the pupils' names into the relevant column and save. This only has to be done once and the names will appear under every objective.

Record a description of the assessment used and the date of the assessment. Where applicable, the assessment activities in each unit of the book can be used to provide the evidence required to help teachers form an accurate picture of each pupil's progress. For example, page 10 presents an assessment activity based on the C1 objective and could be used as part of the evaluation.

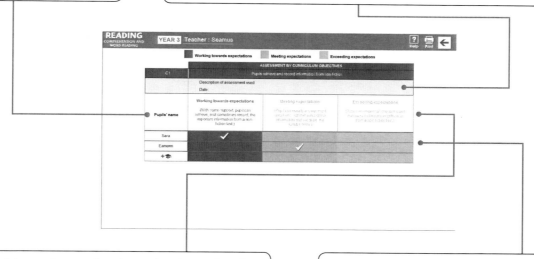

Read the advice and support under each category heading.

Click the box that best applies to each pupil's performance in relation to that objective.

To see a pupil's progress on the curriculum objectives that have been assessed to date, click the pupil's name and the following overview screen will be displayed:

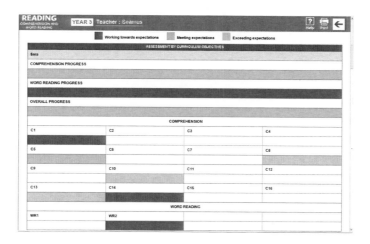

On this screen, which may be printed, the pupil's name is displayed. Progress in both comprehension and word reading are indicated by means of the appropriate colour. An overall progress colour is also displayed. Each curriculum code is displayed at the bottom of this page and the pupil's attainment in relation to this objective is indicated through the relevant colour. This allows teachers to see at a glance the objectives that require additional work.

2. Units in *Reading – Comprehension and Word Reading*

- Click **Assessment by units** in *Reading – Comprehension and Word Reading* on the home page.

- Type in pupils' names.

  (a) Click on the required unit. For example, by clicking on **Unit 1** the codes of the objectives to be assessed in that unit will appear at the top.

  The pupils' names appear down the left-hand side. For each pupil, click the colour that best matches their achievement in relation to that objective. On returning to the page, an average score for that particular unit is displayed (as red, orange or green).

  (b) Click on **FA1**, **FA2** or **FA3**, once the pupils have completed the relevant formal assessment. The following screen will be displayed.

  Click each question the pupil got correct. A tick mark will be generated. Any questions that are not clicked (i.e. the incorrect ones) automatically receive an incorrect mark. The colour in the overall total bar at the base of the page indicates the pupil's performance.

  (c) Click on **TERM** at the end of each term. An end-of-term overview will be displayed, showing a performance colour for both comprehension and word reading.

  An overall average is also displayed, showing the combined progress in both comprehension and word reading. The results of the formal assessment for that term are also displayed on this screen. This screen can be printed for use in either pupil profile folders or parent-teacher meetings.

  (d) Click on **End-of-Year** at the end of the school year. This will display each pupil's overall progress for the entire school year. A breakdown of progress for each term is displayed, as well as progress in comprehension and word reading over the three terms. An overall average is also generated. This entire page can be printed out and passed on to the next teacher of this pupil.

Three summative assessment units are included in each book, for pupils to take after every six units, or at the teacher's discretion.

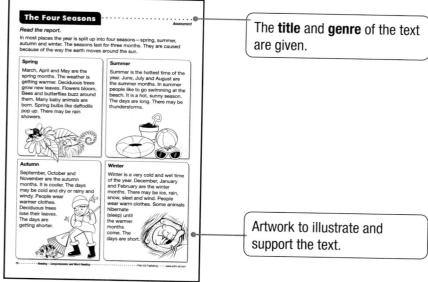

The **title** and **genre** of the text are given.

The tests are based on the National Curriculum assessment guidelines.

Artwork to illustrate and support the text.

Comprehension Assessment

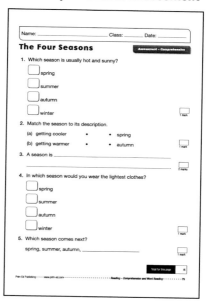

Word Reading Assessment

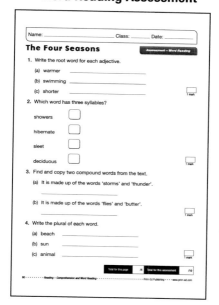

Each question is awarded a mark to a total of 10 marks across the two pages. Inferential questions and multi-part questions are awarded a higher mark than literal questions. Pupils' scores can be recorded on the **Pupil Record Sheet** on page xii. The results of each test can also be recorded on the digital download.

A **Teacher Information** page is provided to accompany each assessment unit.

The **title** and **genre** of the text are given.

The **breakdown of question type/content** and the **mark allocation** are provided in a table. Teachers might choose to photocopy this table for each pupil, ticking/circling the questions answered correctly and recording the marks gained in each assessment and overall.

Answers are provided. Some questions are open-ended and will need to be checked by the teacher.

Text Genres

Unit	Fiction or Non-fiction?	Genre
1. The Magpie's Nest	fiction	folk tale
2. Birds of a Feather	non-fiction	poem
3. The Cold Lad of Hilton	fiction	fairy tale
4. What is a Plant?	non-fiction	report
5. Teeny-Tiny	fiction	fairy tale
6. The Child in the Loft	fiction	poem
7. Lizzy Lizard's Adventure	fiction	poem
8. Eton Mess	non-fiction	recipe
9. Hedgehogs	non-fiction	report
10. The Cheeses that Ran Away	fiction	folk tale
11. The Rowan and the Pine	fiction	narrative
12. Bonfire Night	fiction	narrative
13. Creatures of the Oceans	non-fiction	report
14. Sunbeams	non-fiction	poem
15. How to Make Porridge	non-fiction	recipe
16. The Pedlar of Swaffham	fiction	folk tale
17. The Strange Visitor	fiction	folk tale
18. The Field of Weeds	fiction	folk tale

Word Reading Concepts

Unit 1:	The Magpie's Nest	singular and plural	syllables	short 'e'	
Unit 2:	Birds of a Feather	contractions	'ir' words		
Unit 3:	The Cold Lad of Hilton	suffix '-ed'	suffix '-ing'	'-tch' words	
Unit 4:	What is a Plant?	syllables	plurals '-s' and '-es'	'er' words	
Unit 5:	Teeny-Tiny	suffix '-er'	suffix '-est'	compound words	'ee' words
Unit 6:	The Child in the Loft	'ue' words	'-air' words		
Unit 7:	Lizzy Lizard's Adventure	'-zz' words	'-ll' words	rhyming words	'ai' words
Unit 8:	Eton Mess	singular and plural	plurals with '-es'	compound words	double letters
Unit 9:	Hedgehogs	word meanings	syllables	suffixes '-er', '-est', '-s' and '-es'	'au' words
Unit 10:	The Cheeses that Ran Away	'ar' sound	singular and plural		
Unit 11:	The Rowan and the Pine	nouns	syllables	'aw' words	'ew' words
Unit 12:	Bonfire Night	'-ss' words	suffixes '-ed', '-er' and '-est'	'-tch' words	'igh' words
Unit 13:	Creatures of the Oceans	prefix 'un-'	consonant blends	syllables	
Unit 14:	Sunbeams	rhyming words	compound words	suffixes '-er' and '-est'	'ur' words
Unit 15:	How to Make Porridge	'nk' words	syllables	'oa' words	'ew' words
Unit 16:	The Pedlar of Swaffham	'-tch' words	suffix '-ed'	'ea' words	
Unit 17:	The Strange Visitor	syllables	'-y' words	vocabulary (body)	
Unit 18:	The Field of Weeds	'aw' words	'ie' words	homophones and near-homophones	

Curriculum Objectives and Codes

The following table shows the word reading and comprehension objectives from the reading domain of the English programmes of study. Each objective has been assigned a code. These codes are used throughout the book to assist teachers in planning their work. They are also used in the **Curriculum Links** and **Assessment** tables of the **Teacher Pages**.

Word Reading

WR1	Pupils apply phonic knowledge and skills as the route to decode words.
WR2	Pupils respond speedily with the correct sound to graphemes for all 40+ phonemes, including, where applicable, alternative sounds for graphemes.
WR3	Pupils read accurately by blending sounds in unfamiliar words containing GPCs that have been taught.
WR4	Pupils read common exception words, noting unusual correspondences between spelling and sound and where these occur in the word.
WR5	Pupils read words containing taught GPCs and -s, -es, -ing, -ed, -er and -est endings.
WR6	Pupils read other words of more than one syllable that contain taught GPCs.
WR7	Pupils read words with contractions and understand that the apostrophe represents the omitted letter(s).
WR8	Pupils read aloud accurately books that are consistent with their developing phonic knowledge and that do not require them to use other strategies to work out words.
WR9	Pupils re-read these books to build up their fluency and confidence in word reading.

Comprehension

	Pupils should be taught to develop pleasure in reading, motivation to read, vocabulary and understanding by:
C1	Listening to and discussing a wide range of poems, stories and non-fiction at a level beyond that at which they can read independently.
C2	Being encouraged to link what they read or hear read to their own experiences.
C3	Becoming very familiar with key stories, fairy stories and traditional tales, retelling them and considering their particular characteristics.
C4	Recognising and joining in with predictable phrases.
C5	Learning to appreciate rhymes and poems, and to recite some by heart.
C6	Discussing word meanings, linking new meanings to those already known.
	Pupils should be taught to understand both the books they can already read accurately and fluently and those they listen to by:
C7	Drawing on what they already know or on background information and vocabulary provided by the teacher.
C8	Checking that the text makes sense to them as they read and correcting inaccurate reading.
C9	Discussing the significance of the title and events.
C10	Making inferences on the basis of what is being said and done.
C11	Predicting what might happen on the basis of what has been read so far.
	Pupils should be taught to:
C12	Participate in discussion about what is read to them, taking turns and listening to what others say.
C13	Explain clearly their understanding of what is read to them.

Summative Assessment Units

The following table should be used to record pupils' scores on the three summative assessment units.

Summative Assessment									
	Henny Penny			The Four Seasons			The Beast Inside the Window		
Pupils' names	Comprehension (___/6) Date:	Word Reading (___/4) Date:	TOTAL (___/10) Date:	Comprehension (___/6) Date:	Word Reading (___/4) Date:	TOTAL (___/10) Date:	Comprehension (___/6) Date:	Word Reading (___/4) Date:	TOTAL (___/10) Date:

The following table should be used to record pupils' formative and summative assessments each term.

Pupils' names	Brief Description of Assessments Used		Red — Working towards expectations — Date:	Orange — Meeting expectations — Date:	Green — Exceeding expectations — Date:																	
	Formative	Summative																				

Year: **Term:**

The Magpie's Nest

Curriculum Links

Activity	Code	Objective	Outcome
Text	C1	• Listen to and discuss a wide range of stories at a level beyond that at which they can read independently	• Can discuss their own knowledge and experience of birds and their nests
	C2	• Be encouraged to link what they read or hear read to their own experiences	• Can recognise repeated/predictable phrases
	C4	• Recognise and join in with predictable phrases	• Can discuss the main points of the folk tale
	C12	• Participate in discussion about what is read to them, taking turns and listening to what others say	
Comprehension	C7	• Draw on what they already know or on background information and vocabulary provided by the teacher	• Can explain vocabulary such as 'twig' and 'cooing'
	C9	• Discuss the significance of the title and events	• Can discuss the title and how it relates to the folk tale
	C10	• Make inferences on the basis of what is being said and done	• Can infer why characters feel the way they do
Word Reading	WR1	• Apply phonic knowledge and skills as the route to decode words	• Can get the singular and plural of certain words
	WR2	• Respond speedily with the correct sound to graphemes	• Can read words with the short 'e' sound
	WR6	• Read other words of more than one syllable that contain taught GPCs	• Can use and divide words into syllables

Additional Teacher Information

Definition of Terms

Title
The name of a book, composition or other artistic work.

Text
A book or other written or printed work, regarded in terms of its content rather than its physical form.

Folk tale
A folk tale is a story passed from one generation to the next by word of mouth rather than being written down. A folk tale may include sayings, superstitions, social rituals and legends or lore about the weather, animals or plants.

Links to other Curriculum Areas

• Science – Animals, including humans (Identify and name a variety of common birds)

Terminology for Pupils

folk tale
sentence
word
title
text
syllable
sound

Suggested Reading

• *The Magpie's Nest* by William Stobbs (a picture book version of the tale). This is a vintage book that may be difficult to find.
• *The Magpies' Nest* by Joanna Foster
• *The Birdwatchers* by Simon James

Text

Teacher Information

- This folk tale tells how and why birds build their nests differently.
- During discussion of the text, encourage pupils to employ courteous listening skills such as turn-taking and listening to other pupils' points of view.

Introduction

- Show pictures of birds the pupils may already be familiar with (robin, dove, blue tit and pigeon). An Internet image search should provide very clear pictures. Show pictures of birds from the folk tale: magpie, thrush, blackbird, owl, sparrow, starling and turtle dove. Discuss simple characteristics and lead the conversation to nests. Ask pupils if they have ever seen one. How do they think a bird builds a nest? Discuss the difficulty of building a nest considering birds have no hands to do this.

Development

- Read and discuss the text with pupils, as a whole class, and discuss the text with the pupils to gauge their understanding of what they have listened to or read. Encourage pupils to utilise phonic knowledge and skills while reading so that decoding becomes automatic and reading more fluent. Correct inaccuracies during reading and question pupils to ensure they are making sense of the text. Highlight common exception words so pupils become more familiar with these, which will aid fluency. While reading, observe to see how pupils use phonic skills and knowledge to decode words. Assist those having difficulty decoding words.
- Ensure pupils can read common exception words in this folk tale such as 'enough', 'around', 'said', 'feathers' and 'angrily'.
- After reading the text, ask the pupils to create a step-by-step account of how a bird builds a nest. Record this on the board.

Differentiated Individual/Paired/Group Work

- Work in small groups with less able readers to help them decode words they are having difficulty with.
- More able pupils could work in groups and reread the story. They should be encouraged to read aloud the lines of the different birds with different voices, intonation and expression. They should be encouraged to read aloud to match the emotions of the birds (e.g. Magpie speaks angrily towards the end of the text).

Review

- Assign different pupils the job of reading the lines of different birds. Have one pupil act as narrator and read the lines containing no speech. Each pupil must read their line at the correct time.

Comprehension

Teacher Information

- Questions 8 and 9 provide a good opportunity for the class to discuss friends and feelings. They also provide opportunities to discuss how someone's feelings can be hurt and what might be done to rectify this.

Introduction

- Ask pupils to retell the main events of the folk tale. Encourage them to remember the different birds in the story.
- Reread the story with the pupils one more time.

Development

- Read and discuss the comprehension activities on page 6, then allow pupils to complete the page independently.

Differentiated Individual/Paired/Group Work

- Ask more able pupils to pick their favourite bird from the folk tale and find out some information from nature books or a children's encyclopaedia.
- The teacher can work with a small group of less able readers to ask them to orally summarise the story. The teacher can help them with the sequencing of the events.

Review

- As a class, review questions 8 and 9 and discuss how we all need to listen to each other and also how we should always be respectful to others. Use the story to illustrate these skills.

Word Reading

Teacher Information

- The activities on page 7 focus on singular and plural, syllables and words containing the short 'e' sound.

Introduction

- Reread the text, but first explain to pupils that the focus will be on words. While reading, ask pupils to find and circle words ending in '-s'. After the reading, ask the pupils to read out the words that they found.

Development

- Write some words from the story on the board (or use words recently studied) and ensure that the words chosen are singular. Establish with the pupils that these words refer to one thing only. Introduce that this means these words are singular. Orally demonstrate how these words can be made plural by placing these words in sentences; e.g. word 'bike', sentence 'My friend has two bikes'. Ask pupils if they hear what has changed in the word. Explain to them that these words are plural. Explain that the most common way to make a word plural is to add an '-s' onto the end.

- Using words already known, discuss how the pupils can count syllables in a word. Demonstrate using words (e.g. 'win/dow', 'spi/der', 'pen/cil'). Have pupils clap the syllables in words.

- The short 'e' sound should be spoken out loud, so pupils can hear the sound clearly. Have pupils find other words from the folk tale with the short 'e' sound.

- Discuss the word reading activities on page 7, then allow pupils to complete the page independently.

Differentiated Individual/Paired/Group Work

- In pairs, have pupils write the plurals of the following words: cat, sweet, book, pencil, window, spider, apple, banana, jumper, carpet. Then have them examine the words for syllables.

- More able readers could be challenged to divide the following words into syllables: robin, bank, butterfly, potato, afternoon, triangle, eleven, candle, nose, planet.

- Less able readers may need specific help from the teacher in small groups, particularly with the short 'e' sound. While the other groups are working, have pupils read and practise words such as web, pen, vest, went, bend, spell, deck, neck, shell.

Review

- As a class, have pupils discuss the plurals and syllables they made when they were working in pairs.

	Assessment
C2	Pupils should write three sentences about birds and their nests.
C7	Present the following list of words to the pupils and ask them to write each one in a sentence, showing the meaning of the word: nest, twig, feather
WR1	Present the following list of words to the pupils and ask them to write the plural of each: nest, twig, feather, circle

Answers

Comprehension

1. Answers will vary.
2. Once upon a time
3. (a) I can make a nest now.
   (b) He flew off to make a nest.
4. two, coo
5. nest
6. branch/stick
7. The Magpie's Nest
8. Turtle Dove kept cooing.
9. No
10. Teacher check

Word Reading

1. birds, twigs, feathers
2. owls, magpies, blackbirds, sparrows
3. bird   twig   feather   nest
4. (a) twigs   (b) birds   (c) feather
5. (a) 2   (b) 1   (c) 3
6. mag/pie   work/ing   tur/tle   an/gry
7. Owl and Thrush
8. said, nest, feathers, them
9. (a) best   (b) belt   (c) bell

The Magpie's Nest – 1

Read the folk tale.

Once upon a time, only Magpie knew how to make a nest.

'Show us how to build a nest', said the other birds.

Magpie got some mud. She made a circle with it.

'I can make a nest now', said Thrush. He flew off to make a nest.

Magpie got some twigs. She put them around the mud.

'I can make a nest now', said Blackbird. He flew off to make a nest.

Magpie got more mud. She put it on top of the twigs.

'I can make a nest now', said Owl. He flew off to make a nest.

Magpie took more twigs. She put them around the mud.

'I can make a nest now', said Sparrow. He flew off to make a nest.

Magpie got feathers and grass. She put them in the nest.

'I can make a nest now', said Starling. He flew off to make a nest.

Magpie kept on working. She put one twig
on her nest.

'Take two! Coo! Coo!' said Turtle Dove.

'One is enough!' said Magpie.

'Take two! Coo! Coo!' said Turtle Dove.

'One is enough!' said Magpie angrily.
Turtle Dove kept on cooing.

At last, Magpie got so angry she flew
off. She did not tell any more birds
how to build nests.

My learning log	When I read this folk tale, I could read:	☐ all of it. ☐ most of it. ☐ parts of it.

The Magpie's Nest – 2

1. Tick the birds you have seen, heard or know.

   magpie ☐   thrush ☐   blackbird ☐   owl ☐

   sparrow ☐   starling ☐   turtle dove ☐

2. Write the words that begin most folk and fairy tales.

   _____

3. Circle the sentences that are used often.

   (a) I can make a nest now.   (b) He flew off to make a nest.

   (c) Magpie got some mud.   (d) Turtle Dove kept on cooing.

4. Which words that Turtle Dove said rhyme? _____

5. A place where birds live is called a _____.

6. A twig is a little _____.

7. The title of the text is _____.

8. What happened to make Magpie angry?

   _____

9. Was Turtle Dove being mean to Magpie? Colour. | Yes | No |

10. Draw a picture of the nest Turtle Dove will make.

My learning log	While doing these activities:		
	I found Q _____ easy.	I found Q _____ tricky.	I found Q _____ fun.

6 • • • • • • • • *Reading – Comprehension and Word Reading* •Prim-Ed Publishing • • • • www.prim-ed.com

The Magpie's Nest – 3

1. Circle the words that say more than one.

   birds   twigs   nest   mud   feathers   circle

2. Write 's' onto the end of each word to make more than one.

   owl_____   magpie_____   blackbird_____   sparrow_____

3. Write these words so that they say one.

   birds _____   twigs _____

   feathers _____   nests _____

4. Circle the correct word in each sentence.

   (a) I saw a lot of [twig   twigs] on the ground.

   (b) Paul feeds all the [bird   birds] every day.

   (c) There was one [feather   feathers] in the nest.

5. How many syllables in: (a) enough? ▢ (b) now? ▢ (c) angrily? ▢

6. Split these words into syllables.

   magpie _____   working _____

   turtle _____   angry _____

7. Read the story and write down two birds that have only one syllable

   in their name. _____ and _____

8. Circle the words with a short 'e' sound.

   | said | nest | she |
   | flew | feathers | them |

9. Look at the word 'nest'. Follow the clues to make other short 'e' words.

   (a) Change the first letter to 'b'.   _____

   (b) Now change the third letter to an 'l'.   _____

   (c) Now change the last letter to another 'l'.   _____

My learning log	Colour:	I know what singular and plural mean.	yes / no
		I can divide some words into syllables.	yes / no
		I can read words like 'nest', 'them' and 'said'.	yes / no

Curriculum Links

Activity	Code	Objective	Outcome
Text	C1 C5	• Listen to and discuss a wide range of poems, stories and non-fiction at a level beyond that at which they can read independently • Learn to appreciate rhymes and poems, and to recite some by heart	• Can read and discuss a poem • Can identify rhyming words in a poem
Comprehension	C6 C10	• Discuss word meanings, linking new meanings to those already known • Make inferences on the basis of what is being said and done	• Can understand and use selected vocabulary • Can use a poem to answer questions
Word Reading	WR1 WR2 WR7	• Apply phonic knowledge and skills as the route to decode words • Respond speedily with the correct sound to graphemes • Read words with contractions (for example, I'm, I'll, we'll), and understand that the apostrophe represents the omitted letter(s)	• Can read words with 'ir' like 'bird' • Can read words with contractions (such as can't, that's, I've and I'm)

Additional Teacher Information

Definition of Terms

Poem
A piece of writing in which the expression of feelings and ideas is given intensity by particular attention to diction (sometimes involving rhyme), rhythm and imagery.

Title
The name of a book, composition or other artistic work.

Contraction
A shortened form of a word or group of words; e.g. 'they're' is a contraction of 'they are'.

Non-fiction
Prose writing that is informative or factual rather than fictional.

Links to other Curriculum Areas

• Science – Animals, including humans (describe the structure of a variety of common animals; explore and answer questions about animals in their local environment)

Terminology for Pupils

poem
fact
word
title
sentence
contraction
letter
bracket
sound

Suggested Reading

• *What Makes a Bird a Bird?* by May Garelick
• *Feathers for Lunch* by Lois Ehlert
• *Birds* by Kevin Henkes
• *A Nest Full of Eggs (Let's-Read-and-Find-Out Science, Stage 1)* by Priscilla Belz Jenkins

Text

Teacher Information

- This is a poem about birds and the role of their feathers. It would be useful to do this unit after Unit 1 'The Magpie's Nest' and to discuss both together.

Introduction

- Use an Internet search engine to show pictures of feathers (pick birds the pupils are very familiar with). Ask pupils to suggest reasons why birds have feathers. Ask them if they think birds lose their feathers. Are they born with them? Ask them to generate any questions they may have about feathers.

Development

- Read and discuss the poem with the pupils. Assist them with any unfamiliar words. Question pupils to gauge their understanding of what they have listened to or read. Encourage pupils to utilise phonic knowledge and skills while reading so that decoding becomes automatic and reading more fluent. Correct inaccuracies during reading and question pupils to ensure they are making sense of the text. Highlight common exception words so pupils become more familiar with these, which will aid fluency. While reading, observe to see how pupils use phonic skills and knowledge to decode words. Assist those having difficulty decoding words.

- During reading or listening to the poem, emphasise rhyming words and expression so the pupils can observe and hear fluent and confident reading.

- After reading, discuss difficult words such as 'prey', 'moult' and 'steer'. Ensure pupils understand the meaning of each word.

- Ask pupils to suggest the reasons birds have feathers as mentioned in the poem.

Differentiated Individual/Paired/Group Work

- Ask less able readers to underline all the words that rhyme and then write them in pairs.

- More able readers could write a list of reasons why birds have feathers.

Review

- Sum up the class discussion and the points the pupils have raised in the discussion.

Comprehension

Teacher Information

- The activities and questions on page 12 require that pupils have read the poem carefully and are comfortable with the vocabulary contained within.

Introduction

- Reread the poem and ask pupils some review questions such as: How do feathers help birds in cold weather?/warm weather? Can feathers help birds move? How do feathers keep birds safe? What is the word that means that birds lose old feathers? How do birds get a boyfriend?/girlfriend?

Development

- Read and discuss the comprehension activities on page 12, then allow pupils to complete the page independently. Assist those pupils who find certain questions difficult.

Differentiated Individual/Paired/Group Work

- Ask pupils to work in groups. Give each group an A3 piece of paper/card. Have them create a 'Birds need feathers because …' poster. They can write down any reasons why birds need feathers on lined paper and stick these onto the poster. They can then illustrate each reason. (If they have completed Unit 1 'The Magpie's Nest', they could add in some information on birds' nests.)

Review

- Ask each group to show and discuss their poster. Have the class give a mark out of 10 for each poster. Display the posters on a notice board.

Word Reading

Teacher Information

• The activities on page 13 focus on contractions and 'ir' in words, like 'bird', 'girl' and 'circle'.

Introduction

• Reread the text, but first explain to the pupils that the focus will be on words. While reading, ask pupils to underline any colours mentioned in the poem (brown, black, red, orange, yellow).

Development

• Write the words 'can't', 'I'm' and 'I've' on the board. Ask pupils to find these in the poem. Explain that these words are really two words shortened into one. Demonstrate this with each of the words. Explain that the apostrophe is used to show that letters are missing. Tell pupils that words that are shortened like this are called contractions. Give plenty of examples and allow pupils to make up their own sentences using these contractions. Each time, make sure that they can explain what letters are left out to form the contraction.

• The 'ir' in 'bird' should be exaggerated and spoken out loud, so pupils are aware of how this sounds in words. When correcting question 4, ensure that the 'ir' is exaggerated.

• Discuss the word reading activities on page 13, then allow pupils to complete the page independently.

Differentiated Individual/Paired/Group Work

• Challenge more able readers to use the 'ir' words from question 4 in sentences, using two or more 'ir' words in the one sentence. If the pupils can come up with any other words like these, they can put them in a list.

• Have pupils create a poster of common contractions that they will encounter in Year 1. Have them divide the poster into three columns and write the contraction in the first column, the full words it is shortened from in the second column, and in the final column the letter(s) left out. Encourage them to use colour to make the poster visually appealing.

Review

• Bring the whole class together and revise the main points of the lesson. Ensure that all pupils know the term contraction and that they can recognise, read and tell what words are shortened in common contractions.

Assessment

C1/5	Have the pupils read aloud the poem on page 11 individually (have the rest of the class working on a different task). Ensure that each pupil can read the poem with fluency and can read the words correctly. Note this as part of the assessment. If a pupil is having difficulty with sounding out words, note this also. To check that they understand rhyme, ask them to find the rhyming words in the poem for 'away' ('prey'), 'year' ('appear') and 'steer' ('near').
WR1	Ask pupils to spell the words from question 4 on page 13 on a blank sheet of paper. The focus of this assessment should be if they can represent the 'ir' correctly. Note the pupils who can spell the full word correctly.
WR7	Ask pupils to fill in an assessment grid such as the following:

words	contraction	letter(s) left out
I am		
we will		
I have		

Answers

Comprehension

1. rhyming
2. information
3. Birds, Feather
4. (a) moult   (b) prey
5. Answers will vary.
6. Answers will vary.
7. forest, wood
8. They use their tail feathers to steer.
9. Feathers help to camouflage the bird./They are the same colour as leaves, bushes or trees so they can't be seen.
10. feathers

Word Reading

1. can't, that's, I'm, there's, I've
2. (a) I have; h, a
   (b) I am; a
   (c) there is; i
3. (a) That's (b) I've (c) can't (d) there's
4. (a) girl (b) shirt (c) first (d) third
   (e) birthday (f) circus (g) stir (h) circle
5. (a) birthday (b) first (c) third
   (d) circus (e) shirt, circle

Birds of a Feather – 1

Read the non-fiction poem.

Birds wear very funny clothes.

They have feathers from their nose to their toes.

Birds are the only animals covered with feathers.

They use them in all kinds of weather.

Feathers keep them warm and dry

But best of all they help birds fly!

Feathers on their tail help them steer

From left to right, from far to near.

Feathers help birds to hide away

So they can't become someone's prey.

Birds fluff up their feathers when they want to look good

To get a boyfriend or girlfriend from their forest or wood.

Feathers come in every colour, you know.

They can be brown, black, red, orange or yellow.

Birds lose old feathers once or twice a year

But after they moult, new feathers appear.

Feathers protect birds from sunburn.

That's what I've heard.

But there's one fact of which I'm sure.

You must have feathers to be a bird!

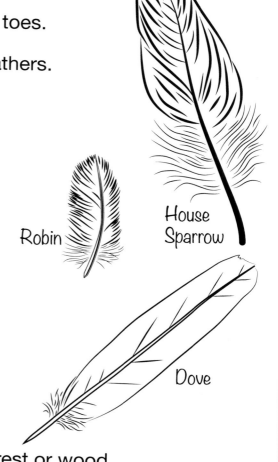

Robin

House Sparrow

Dove

Starling

| My learning log | When I read this poem, I could read: | ☐ all of it. ☐ most of it. ☐ parts of it. |

Birds of a Feather – 2

1. Colour the correct answer.

   Many poems have ⟨ rhyming ⟩ ⟨ rhyme ⟩ words at the end of each line.

2. This poem gives facts or i_____.

3. Which two words in the title tell what the poem is about?

   • _____   • _____

4. Which word means:

   (a) 'to lose old feathers'?   _____

   (b) 'an animal hunted for food'?   _____

5. Write one other fact you know about birds. _____

   _____

6. What would happen if birds did not have feathers? _____

   _____

7. Write two places birds live.

   _____

8. What do birds do when they are flying and want to go another way?

   _____

9. How do feathers help birds hide from prey?

   _____

   _____

10. Finish the sentence.

    A bird is an animal with _____.

My learning log	While doing these activities:		
	I found Q _____ easy.	I found Q _____ interesting.	I found Q _____ difficult.

Birds of a Feather – 3

1. Circle the words below that are contractions.

| can't | they | that's | I'm | there's | what | I've | all |

2. On the first line, write the two words that make up the contraction. On the second line, write the letters that are left out.

(a) I've _____   _____

(b) I'm _____   _____

(c) there's _____   _____

3. Change the words in brackets into a contraction.

(a) (That is) _____ all the money I have.

(b) I think (I have) _____ seen this film before.

(c) Mum said I (cannot) _____ go outside until I finish my homework.

(d) Do you know if (there is) _____ any milk left?

4. Add 'ir' like in 'bird' to these words. Read each word.

(a) g____l   (b) sh____t   (c) f____st   (d) th____d

(e) b____thday   (f) c____cus   (g) st____   (h) c____cle

5. Fill in the missing words. Use the words in question 4 to help you.

(a) The _____ cake had chocolate icing.

(b) My sister won the race so she got the _____ prize.

(c) My cousin didn't come second but she came in _____ place.

(d) Dad said we can go to the _____ after school.

(e) The blue _____ had a red _____ on the sleeve.

My learning log	Colour:	I know what a contraction is.	yes / no
		I know what two words *I've* is made from.	yes / no
		If I see 'ir' in a word, I can say its sound.	yes / no
		I can read words like 'circle', 'girl', 'third' and 'shirt'.	yes / no

Curriculum Links

Activity	Code	Objective	Outcome
Text	C1	• Listen to and discuss a wide range of stories at a level beyond that at which they can read independently	• Can discuss the features of a fairy tale
	C3	• Become very familiar with fairy stories and traditional tales, retelling them and considering their particular characteristics	• Can read and explain words such as 'servants', 'vanished' and 'rooster'
	C6	• Discuss word meanings, linking new meanings to those already known	
Comprehension	C8	• Check that the text makes sense to them as they read and correct inaccurate reading	• Can demonstrate understanding of the fairy tale
	C10	• Make inferences on the basis of what is being said or done	• Can infer why characters did/felt certain things
	C13	• Explain clearly their understanding of what is read to them	
Word Reading	WR1	• Apply phonic knowledge and skills as the route to decode words	• Can read '-tch' words
	WR4	• Read common exception words, noting unusual correspondences between spelling and sound and where these occur in the word	• Can read some common exception words
	WR5	• Read words containing -ing and -ed endings	• Can add '-ed' and '-ing' to words

Additional Teacher Information

Definition of Terms

Title
The name of a book, composition or other artistic work.

Story
An account of imaginary or real people and events told for entertainment.

Text
A book or other written or printed work, regarded in terms of its content rather than its physical form.

Fairy tale
A fairy tale is a short story usually featuring fantasy characters such as elves, dragons, hobgoblins, sprites or magical beings and often set in the distant past. A fairy tale usually begins with the phrase 'Once upon a time ...' and ends with the words '... and they lived happily ever after'. Charms, disguises and talking animals may also appear in a fairy tale.

Terminology for Pupils

fairy tale
title
word
event
story
text

Suggested Reading

- *The Brownies and Other Stories* by Mrs Ewing
- *The Enid Blyton Book of Brownies* by Enid Blyton
- *The Brownies and their Book* by Palmer Cox

Text

Teacher Information

- A house elf is a benevolent elf that supposedly haunts houses and does housework secretly.

- In some versions of this tale, the house elf was under a magic spell that could only be broken if he was given a gift. By playing tricks on everyone he hoped someone would notice and help him.

- In many stories, the 'hen-wife' (woman who looked after the hens) was old and wise and sometimes had supernatural powers.

Introduction

- Tell pupils they are going to read a fairy tale about a house elf. Ask them if they have ever heard about them. If not, give a quick overview of the information contained above.

Development

- Read and discuss the fairy tale with the pupils. Assist them with any unfamiliar words. Encourage pupils to utilise phonic knowledge and skills while reading so that decoding becomes automatic and reading more fluent. Correct inaccuracies during reading and question pupils to ensure they are making sense of the text. Highlight common exception words so pupils become more familiar with these to aid fluency. While reading, observe to see how pupils use phonic skills and knowledge to decode words. Assist those having difficulty decoding words. Ensure that pupils understand any of the difficult vocabulary.

- After reading, have a discussion about what they think of the house elf. Is he good? Did he do things that weren't nice? Did he do things that were helpful? Why did he go away? Why did the servants want to help him?

Differentiated Individual/Paired/Group Work

- Have pupils work in pairs. Ask them to discuss the main events of the story. They should work together to create a picture board of the events. Each picture must tell a major event/happening in the story. This might take a few days to complete.

- More able pupils could add written text to the pictures (to create a comic-like end product).

Review

- Pupils should share their work with the whole class.

Comprehension

Teacher Information

- Question 9 requires pupils to write something else about house elves/brownies. The books in the 'Suggested Reading' section of the 'Teacher Information' notes section would be useful here. Short stories could be read to the pupils at different points during the day.

Introduction

- Pupils take it in turns to retell the fairy tale in their own words, sequencing the events correctly.

- Reread the fairy tale once again, to establish all the finer points of the story.

Development

- Discuss the comprehension activities on page 18, then allow pupils to complete the page independently.

- Compare their answers to questions that may have varied answers, especially questions 6 and 8. Pupils should tell why they chose their answers, based on the events in the fairy tale.

Differentiated Individual/Paired/Group Work

- Ask pupils to use their imaginations to think of other unhelpful things that the house elf could have done at Hilton Hall. They could make a list of these things. Then they could think of helpful things that he could have done to help the servants.

- More able pupils should write a longer list than less able pupils.

Review

- Ask the pupils if they thought the advice given by the woman who looked after the hens was good advice. What else could the servants have made for the house elf? Discuss these questions as a whole class. During the discussion, encourage pupils to employ courteous listening skills such as turn-taking and listening to what others have to say.

Word Reading

Teacher Information

- The activities on page 19 focus on adding '-ed' and '-ing' to words, common exception words and 'tch' in the middle and the end of words.

Introduction

- Reread the text with the class, but first explain to pupils that the focus will be on words. While reading, ask pupils to circle any words ending in '-ing' and '-ed'.

Development

- After reading, ask pupils what words they found. Compile a list on the board under the headings '-ed' and '-ing'. If root words have been covered, revise that the words without the endings are root words. Provide some further examples, bearing in mind that all questions on the activity sheet involve words that do not require a spelling change in the root word before '-ed' or '-ing' is added.

- The question on common exception words requires the pupils to find how many times the words are found in the text. Ensure pupils can read these words before they attempt this question.

- The 'tch' part of words can be found at the end of a word (watch) and in the middle of a word (kitchen). Ensure that time is given to exploring the sound of 'tch' and that pupils can sound it out in medial and final positions. When the pupils have completed question 4 ('tch' in the final position), ask pupils to read out the words carefully. Question 6 examines 'tch' in the medial position of words.

- Question 5 provides further practice of 'tch' words, but focuses the pupil's attention on the preceding vowel sound and changing it to create a new word.

- Pupils complete the word reading activities on page 19 independently.

Differentiated Individual/Paired/Group Work

- Challenge more able readers to use the 'tch' words in questions 4 and 6 in a short paragraph. They need to think about a simple idea that would require the use of a lot of the words in these questions.

- The teacher could work with a group of readers and provide intensive practice on 'tch' words. Encourage them to sound out the initial parts of the words and then add on the 'tch' ending. Once they have had a lot of practice with these, see if they can spell these words. They could place these words into sentences.

Review

- Bring the class back together and ask them to read out some of their work on 'tch' words.

Assessment

C6	Present the following list of words to the pupils and ask them to write a simple sentence that shows the meaning of each word: servants, vanished, rooster, peeped, midnight
C13	With the help of a teacher's assistant, ask the pupils to orally summarise the story. Note down as part of the assessment if the pupil can recall most of the details in the correct order.
WR1	Present pupils with a list written with a blank space followed by '-tch' (e.g. __tch). Call out the following words and have pupils write the missing initial letters: pitch, witch, fetch, watch, catch, match, hutch

Answers

Comprehension

1. The Cold Lad of Hilton
2. Long ago
3. a nut from an (oak) tree
4. (a) cloak   (b) vest/tank top/waistcoat
5. The house elf was singing a sad song.
6. Answers may include: He was naughty./He was trying to get attention.
7. No
8. … jumped about the kitchen happily.
9. Answers will vary.
10. young girl in the Guides Association/a small square of rich chocolate cake, often with nuts

Word Reading

1. (a) turn   (b) help   (c) peep   (d) look
   (e) want   (f) wait   (g) vanish   (h) jump
2. (a) looking   (b) waiting   (c) vanishing
   (d) turning   (e) helping   (f) jumping
3. said/2, he/7, she/1, was/3, do/2, put/3
4. (a) pitch   (b) hutch   (c) catch
   (d) witch   (e) match   (f) hatch
   (g) fetch   (h) patch   (i) watch
5. (a) witch   (b) patch   (c) hutch
6. (a) butcher   (b) kitchen
   (c) ketchup   (d) hatchet

The Cold Lad of Hilton – 1

Read the fairy tale.

Long ago, at a large house called Hilton Hall, there lived a difficult house elf. He turned chairs and tables upside down. He put sugar in the salt dishes. He threw water on the fires and put them out. Sometimes he helped the servants. If a bowl of honey or a cake was left out, the house elf tidied the kitchen.

Late one night, the servants heard a noise in the kitchen. They peeped in. They saw the house elf. He was singing a sad song.

'Woe is me! Woe is me!

The acorn has not yet fallen from the tree,

That will grow into wood,

That will make the cradle,

That will rock the baby,

That will grow to be a man,

That will get rid of me.'

The servants felt sorry for the house elf. They went to the old woman who looked after the hens. They wanted to find out what to do.

'That's easy!' she said. 'A house elf that is paid for its work with anything that will last will go away.'

The servants made a green cloak with a hood. They placed it next to the fire. Then they watched and waited.

Late that night, the house elf came into the kitchen. He saw the cloak and put it on. He jumped about the kitchen happily. When the rooster crowed at dawn, the house elf said,

'Here's a cloak and here's a hood!

The Cold Lad of Hilton will do no more good!'

The house elf vanished and was never seen again.

However, some people say they can still hear the house elf singing his sad song at midnight.

My learning log	When I read this fairy tale, I could read:	☐ all of it. ☐ most of it. ☐ parts of it.

The Cold Lad of Hilton – 2

1. Write the title of the fairy tale.

   _____

2. Which words begin this fairy tale? _____

3. An acorn is _____ .

4. (a) Which word means 'a piece of clothing without sleeves

   that hangs from the shoulders'? _____

   (b) What other clothing has no sleeves? _____

5. What event made the servants feel sorry for the house elf?

   _____

6. Why did the house elf do the things he did?

   _____

7. Do you think there will be sugar in the salt now? | Yes | | No |

8. The house elf was happy to get the cloak because he:

   _____

9. (a) A house elf is also known as a 'brownie'. Write something you know
   about house elves or brownies like the one in the story.

   _____

   _____

   (b) Write the name of another story with a house elf or brownie in it.

   _____

10. A brownie is also a _____ .

My learning log	While doing these activities:		
	I found Q _____ easy.	I found Q _____ tricky.	I found Q _____ fun.

The Cold Lad of Hilton – 3

1. Write the word before '-ed' was added.

   (a) turned _____   (b) helped _____

   (c) peeped _____   (d) looked _____

   (e) wanted _____   (f) waited _____

   (g) vanished _____   (h) jumped _____

2. Add '-ing' to these words.

   (a) look _____   (b) wait _____

   (c) vanish _____   (d) turn _____

   (e) help _____   (f) jump _____

3. How many times are these words found in the text?

   said ☐   he ☐   she ☐   was ☐   do ☐   put ☐

4. The word 'watch' has '-tch' at the end. Add '-tch' and then read the words.

   (a) pi_____   (b) hu_____   (c) ca_____

   (d) wi_____   (e) ma_____   (f) ha_____

   (g) fe_____   (h) pa_____   (i) wa_____

5. Follow the instructions. Write the word. Draw a small picture.

   (a) Change the 'a' in 'watch' to an 'i'. _____

   (b) Change the 'i' in 'pitch' to an 'a'. _____

   (c) Change the 'a' in 'hatch' to a 'u'. _____

6. These words have 'tch' in the middle. Fill in the 'tch' and read the words.

   (a) bu_____er   (b) ki_____en   (c) ke_____up   (d) ha_____et

My learning log	Colour:	I can add '-ed' and '-ing' onto words.	yes / no
		I can read words with 'tch' like 'witch', 'match' and 'kitchen'.	yes / no
	Tick if you can read and spell these words.	☐ said ☐ was ☐ put	

What is a Plant?

Curriculum Links

Activity	Code	Objective	Outcome
Text	C1	• Listen to and discuss a wide range of non-fiction at a level beyond that at which they can read independently	• Can read a report and say what they have learned
	C6	• Discuss word meanings, linking new meanings to those already known	• Can tell the meaning of words such as 'branches', 'nutrients' and 'oxygen'
Comprehension	C7	• Draw on what they already know or on background information and vocabulary provided by the teacher	• Can discuss some of the main points raised in a report
	C9	• Discuss the significance of the title and events	• Can understand the parts of a report
Word Reading	WR2	• Respond speedily with the correct sound to graphemes for all 40+ phonemes, including, where applicable, alternative sounds for graphemes	• Can read words with 'er' like 'flower'
	WR5	• Read words containing -s and -es endings	• Can add '-s' and '-es' to words to make them plural

Additional Teacher Information

Definition of Terms

Title
The name of a book, composition or other artistic work.

Text
A book or other written or printed work, regarded in terms of its content rather than its physical form.

Report
A report is a written document describing the findings of an individual or group. A report may take the form of a newspaper report, sports or police report, or a report about an animal, person or object.

Links to other Curriculum Areas

• Science – Plants (Identify and describe the basic structure of a variety of common flowering plants, including trees; Identify and name a variety of common wild and garden plants, including deciduous and evergreen trees)

Terminology for Pupils

report
title
text
word
syllable

Suggested Reading

• *How Plants Grow (Time for Kids Non-fiction Readers)* by Dona Herweck Rice
• *From Seed to Plant (Rookie Read-About Science)* by Allan Fowler
• *The Tiny Seed (The World of Eric Carle)* by Eric Carle
• *Oh Say Can You Seed?: All About Flowering Plants (Cat in the Hat's Learning Library)* by Bonnie Worth

Text

Teacher Information

- This text is in the form of a report. Discuss with the pupils that a report is written very differently to stories and poems. Explain that the purpose can often be to give information.

Introduction

- When discussing information texts, consider what the pupils may already know about the topic. All pupils will be familiar with plants (and this topic may have been covered in a science lesson; if it has, use the pupils' prior knowledge to revise the topic).

Development

- Read and discuss the text with pupils, as a whole class, and discuss the text with the pupils to gauge their understanding of what they have listened to or read. Encourage pupils to utilise phonic knowledge and skills while reading so that decoding becomes automatic and reading more fluent. Correct inaccuracies during reading and question pupils to ensure they are making sense of the text. Highlight common exception words so pupils become more familiar with these to aid fluency. While reading, observe to see how pupils use phonic skills and knowledge to decode words. Assist those having difficulty decoding words. Ask questions to gauge understanding of vocabulary including 'knobby', 'nutrients', 'energy', 'pollen' and 'attract'. A simple explanation of 'carbon dioxide' may be needed.

- Question pupils to gauge their understanding of what they have listened to or read. Ask questions such as: What do roots do? Why are leaves important? What are seeds? Where do seeds come from? What is another word for the stem? What are buds? Ask more demanding questions such as: What makes a plant different from an animal?

- Ask pupils to come up with some other possible titles this report could have used.

Differentiated Individual/Paired/Group Work

- Provide pupils with a picture of a plant. Ask them to label the flower, the leaf, the stem and the roots. Have more able readers add the job that each of these perform.

Review

- Have the whole class do an oral synopsis of the important information they have learned from the report.

Comprehension

Teacher Information

- Question 1 requires pupils to relate the information to their own lives, asking them to identify plants they have in their own garden or have seen before.

Introduction

- Reread the report. Check to see that pupils remember the key points and vocabulary contained within this report. For example, can they explain buds? ferns? oxygen? carbon dioxide? nutrients? pollen?

Development

- Discuss the comprehension activities on page 24, then allow pupils to complete the page independently.

- Compare their answers to questions that may have varied answers, especially questions 5, 6 and 7. Pupils should be able to give reasons for their answers based on the report.

Differentiated Individual/Paired/Group Work

- Ask more able pupils to write a short report on a tree of their choice (oak, beech, etc.). Encourage them to follow a structure/layout that is similar to the report they have read. Alternatively, encourage them to choose their own headings for each part of the report.

- Have less able pupils write out the five parts of a plant on small flashcards (root, stem, flower, leaf and seed) and on separate strips of paper the jobs these parts do. Then in pairs, have the pupils take their pieces of paper and match each part to its job.

Review

- Bring the whole class together and ask the pupils to summarise the findings they have learned from the report. If they haven't yet covered plants in science, create a class chart on the parts of the plant. They can display this on the wall and use it to revise and revisit the features when starting this topic in science.

Word Reading

Teacher Information

- The activities on page 25 focus on syllables, adding '-s' or '-es' to make singular words plural and words with 'er' such as 'flower'.

Introduction

- Reread the text, but first explain to pupils that the focus will be on words. As they are rereading ask them to underline any plural words that they see with '-es'.

Development

- After rereading the text, ask pupils to contribute the words that they found ending in '-es'. Make a list on the board. Revise with the pupils the terms singular and plural. They will have met these before. Ask them what is the rule for making most words plural (add '-s'). Have them examine the list on the board. Is there any feature that they notice in the words? (a lot end in '-sh' or '-ch'). Explain that words like this need '-es' in the plural. If they have completed Unit 3 ('-tch' words), they can be taught that these words take '-es'. Other words to demonstrate this rule include brush, watch, match, lunch.

- Syllables are covered in question 1. Pupils need to divide the words into the correct syllable boxes. Give them plenty of practice using words previously covered in class.

- Focus on the word 'flower'. Underline or highlight the 'er'. Make sure pupils are comfortable with the 'er' sound.

- Discuss the word reading activities on page 25, then allow pupils to complete the page independently.

Differentiated Individual/Paired/Group Work

- In pairs, one pupil writes a sentence using words from question 2 in the singular. The other pupil must write the same sentence using the plural forms of the words.

- Ask pupils to write some clues for words that have 'er' in them. They can use these words to have a class quiz on 'Guess the 'er' word'.

Review

- Ask the whole class to recap on the main features of the lesson today. If pupils have their 'er' clues ready, finish the lesson by playing 'Guess the 'er' word'.

Assessment

C6	Ask pupils to write the following words in a sentence that shows its meaning:
	herb, nutrient, branch, trunk, attract
	Remind pupils that they can use the words in the singular or in the plural.
C7	Ask pupils to write down five facts they have learned from reading the report.
WR5	Present the pupils with the following list of words. Ask them to write the plural word beside each singular word.
	plant, flower, branch, bush, match, seed, nutrient, lunch, church, stem

Answers

Comprehension

1. Answers will vary.
2. (a) herb–a plant used for cooking
   (b) moss–a low plant without flowers that grows where it is damp
   (c) nutrients–good things that help plants grow
3. (a) roots   (b) stem   (c) flowers
   (d) leaf/leaves   (e) seed/seeds   (f) branch/branches
4. (a) What is a Plant?
   (b) Yes, because it tells exactly what the text is about.
5. No—Plants need the sun to make food.
6. No—Plant roots keep them anchored in the soil.
7. If a plant did not get water, it would probably die.

Word Reading

1. (a) nu/tri/ents   (b) car/ry   (c) liv/ing
2. Add 's': plants, shrubs, insects, flowers, petals
   Add 'es': bushes, branches
3. (a) churches   (b) toys
   (c) cats, dog   (d) wishes
4. (a) her   (b) herb
   (c) person   (d) serve
5. (a) serve   (b) herb

What is a Plant? – 1

Read the report.

What is a plant?

A plant is a living thing. Plants can be many different shapes, colours and sizes. They live in many different places. Trees, grass, shrubs, bushes, herbs, ferns and moss are all plants. Plants cannot move from the place they are growing.

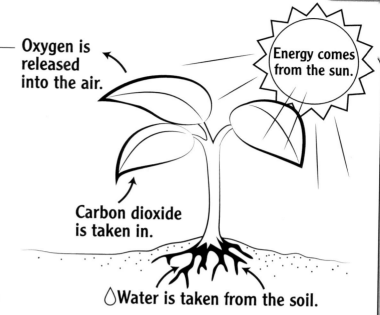

Oxygen is released into the air.

Energy comes from the sun.

Carbon dioxide is taken in.

💧Water is taken from the soil.

What parts does a plant have?

Plants have many different parts. The main parts are roots, stem or trunk, leaves, flowers and branches. Flowers have small parts called petals. Buds are small knobby parts of a plant that grow into a flower, a leaf or both. Many plants start growing from a seed or bulb. The parts of a plant all have a job to do.

What jobs do the parts of a plant have?

Roots hold the plant in the soil so it will not fall over. They suck up water and nutrients for the plant like a straw. Roots can store extra food for later.

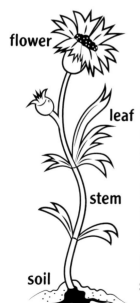

flower

leaf

stem

soil

roots

Stems hold up the plant. They act like pipes to carry water and nutrients around the plant. Stems can bend or be stiff and hard like a tree trunk.

Leaves are the place where food is made. Leaves give off oxygen into the air. They take carbon dioxide from the air, and water and nutrients from the soil, and change them into food.

Flowers are the part of the plant that make the seeds. Some flowers grow into fruit. There are seeds inside fruit. Flower petals and the smell of flowers attract bees and insects. Insects and bees spread pollen that make new seeds.

Seeds grow into new plants.

My learning log	When I read this report, I could read:	☐ all of it.	☐ most of it.	☐ parts of it.

What is a Plant? – 2

1. Tick the plants you have in your garden or have seen before.

   tree ☐   grass ☐   shrub ☐   bush ☐

   fern ☐   herb ☐   moss ☐

2. Match the word to its meaning.

   (a) herb •   • good things that help plants grow

   (b) moss •   • a plant used for cooking

   (c) nutrients •   • a low plant without flowers
                        that grows where it is damp

3. Write the names of six plant parts.

   (a) r_____   (b) st_____   (c) fl_____

   (d) l_____   (e) s_____   (f) br_____

4. (a) What is the title of the text?

   _____

   (b) Is it a good title? ☐ Yes ☐ No Why?

   _____

5. Can plants live without energy from the sun? ☐ Yes ☐ No Why?

   _____

6. Can plants move? ☐ Yes ☐ No Why?

   _____

7. What would happen if a plant did not get water?

   _____

My learning log	While doing these activities:		
	I found Q _____ easy.	I found Q _____ tricky.	I found Q _____ fun.

What is a Plant? – 3

1. Write each word correctly in the syllable boxes.

   (a) nutrients

   (b) carry

   (c) living

2. To make words mean more than one, some words take an '-s' and some words take an '-es'. Write these words from the story in the correct box.

plant   shrub   bush   insect   branch   flower   petal

Add '-s' to make more than one.	Add '-es' to make more than one.

3. Write the correct word on the line.

   (a) I visited three (church) _____ today.

   (b) All the (toy) _____ were missing.

   (c) The nice lady has seven (cat) _____ but only one (dog)

   _____.

   (d) The wizard gave me three (wish) _____.

4. The word 'flower' has 'er'. Write 'er' into these and then read each word.

   (a) h_____   (b) h_____b   (c) p_____son   (d) s_____ve

5. Solve the clues for the words that have 'er'.

   (a) happens in a tennis match   _____

   (b) can be used in cooking   _____

My learning log	*Colour:*	I can count the syllables in words.	yes / no
		I know when to add '-s' and '-es' to make words plural.	yes / no
		I can read 'serve', 'herb' and 'person'.	yes / no

Curriculum Links

Activity	Code	Objective	Outcome
Text	C3 C4	• Become very familiar with fairy stories, retelling them and considering their particular characteristics • Recognise and join in with predictable phrases	• Can retell a fairy tale
Comprehension	C9 C11 C12	• Discuss the significance of the title and events • Predict what might happen on the basis of what has been read so far • Participate in discussion about what is read to them, taking turns and listening to what others say	• Can discuss the fairy tale with others • Can predict what might happen if the fairy tale continued
Word Reading	WR2 WR5	• Respond speedily with the correct sound to graphemes • Read words containing -er and -est endings	• Can read words with 'ee' in them • Can make compound words • Can add '-er' and '-est' to words

Additional Teacher Information

Definition of Terms

Title
The name of a book, composition or other artistic work.

Text
A book or other written or printed work, regarded in terms of its content rather than its physical form.

Story
An account of imaginary or real people and events told for entertainment.

Fairy tale
A fairy tale is a short story usually featuring fantasy characters such as elves, dragons, hobgoblins, sprites or magical beings and often set in the distant past. A fairy tale usually begins with the phrase 'Once upon a time ...' and ends with the words '... and they lived happily ever after'. Charms, disguises and talking animals may also appear in a fairy tale.

Terminology for Pupils

fairy tale
title
text
word
story
adjective
compound word

Suggested Reading

- *In a Dark, Dark Room and Other Scary Stories (I Can Read! Reading 2)* by Alvin Schwartz
- *The Tailypo: A Ghost Story* by Joanna C. Galdone
- *In a Dark, Dark Wood* by David A. Carter

Text

Teacher Information

- Young children enjoy simple, scary stories. The repetitive words and phrases make the story fun and easy to read, and help develop fluency and confidence.

Introduction

- Discuss and help pupils read the words 'teeny-tiny'. Ask pupils why they think this is used instead of 'small' or simply 'tiny'. Explain that this fairy tale is supposed to give a teeny-tiny scare at the end.

Development

- Read and discuss the text with pupils, as a whole class, and discuss the text with the pupils to gauge their understanding of what they have listened to or read. Encourage pupils to utilise phonic knowledge and skills while reading so that decoding becomes automatic and reading more fluent. Correct inaccuracies during reading and question pupils to ensure they are making sense of the text. Highlight common exception words so pupils become more familiar with these to aid fluency. While reading, observe to see how pupils use phonic skills and knowledge to decode words. Assist those having difficulty decoding words.

- After reading, ask pupils to discuss the events in the fairy tale. Focus on the details of the fairy tale and make a list of the main events of the story on the board.

Differentiated Individual/Paired/Group Work

- Have pupils think in pairs about who is saying 'Give me my bone!' Where do they think it came from?

- Ask the pupils to discuss in groups what they think happened at the end.

- More able readers can write a short paragraph saying what they think happened. Less able readers could discuss this in pairs and explain to the teacher what they think happened.

Review

- Bring the whole class together and select a few pupils to share what they think happened at the end of this story.

Comprehension

Teacher Information

- Question 9 asks the pupils if they have read, or heard, a scary story before. Use some of the stories recommended in the 'Suggested Reading' section of the 'Teacher Information'.

Introduction

- Reread the story with the class. Ask simple review questions based on the story: Where did the teeny-tiny woman live? Why did the teeny-tiny woman pick up the bone? Where did the voice come from?

Development

- Discuss the comprehension activities on page 30, then allow pupils to complete the page independently.

- Compare their answers to questions 6, 7 and 8 which will have varied answers. Pupils should explain why they gave a particular answer.

Differentiated Individual/Paired/Group Work

- More able readers could write a paragraph called 'Teeny-Tiny Me'. They could describe where they live using the words 'teeny-tiny'.

- Less able readers could reread the story and draw all the teeny-tiny things mentioned in the fairy tale (e.g. house, gate, grave, graveyard, bone and cupboard). They must write each word over each teeny-tiny picture.

Review

- Have different pupils show their work to the class. Some pupils could read their 'Teeny-Tiny Me' stories. Other pupils could share their pictures of the teeny-tiny things in the stories.

Word Reading

Teacher Information

- The activities on page 31 focus on adding '-er' and '-est' to words, compound words and words with 'ee', such as 'green'.

Introduction

- Reread the text, but first explain to pupils that the focus of the reading will be on words. While reading, ask pupils to underline the words 'graveyard' and 'cupboard' anywhere they occur in the text.

Development

- Discuss with the pupils the endings '-er' and '-est'. Allow plenty of time to discuss, through the use of example sentences, the difference between the two endings.

- Introduce the term compound words. Use the words the pupils underlined in the text, 'graveyard' and 'cupboard', to demonstrate that the two words are separate and have separate meanings. When combined they take on a different meaning. Use other common examples such as 'butterfly', 'armchair', 'lipstick', 'cupcake' and 'cartwheel'.

- Introduce the 'ee' sound found throughout the text in 'teeny'. Highlight the sound to ensure that pupils can sound this out correctly.

- Pupils should complete the word reading activities on page 31 independently.

Differentiated Individual/Paired/Group Work

- More able readers should create sentences showing the difference between '-er' and '-est' words used in questions 1 and 2.

- Less able readers should work on compound words. Ask them to draw pictures of each part of a compound word and insert a '+' sign between them, and then insert an '=' sign and finally a new picture of the new compound word.

e.g.   light   +   house   =   lighthouse

They should write the words under each picture.

Review

- Pupils should read/display some of their work, then revise some of the key points of the lesson.

Assessment

C3/4	Ask pupils to retell the fairy tale in as much detail as they can recall. Note if they can remember the 'Give me my bone!' line that is repeated throughout the fairy tale.
C11	Pupils should write a short paragraph of text to tell what happened after the teeny-tiny woman told the voice to take the teeny-tiny bone.
WR2	Individually test pupils to see if they can read the following ten 'ee' words: feet, meet, seem, weep, teeth, sleep, cheek, sheep, sneeze, between

Answers

Comprehension

1. Teeny-Tiny
2. Everything in the story is described as teeny-tiny.
3. Once upon a time
4. teeny-tiny
5. (a) bone   (b) graveyard
6. Answers may include: the teeny-tiny voice/a skeleton/a ghost/the person who is buried in the grave where the bone was found.
7. Answers may include: the owner of the teeny-tiny voice will take it back to the graveyard. However, teachers should accept any answers that pupils can justify.
8. on the teeny-tiny woman's teeny-tiny bed
9. Answers will vary.
10. Answers may include: food, clothes, linen, kitchen equipment etc.

Word Reading

1. (a) -er   (b) -est
2. (a) slower, slowest   (b) quieter, quietest
   (c) faster, fastest   (d) younger, youngest
   (e) older, oldest
3. grave, yard
4. (a) lighthouse   (b) bedroom   (c) basketball
   (d) goldfish   (e) blackberry
5. (a) green   (b) meet   (c) week   (d) tree
6. (a) greet   (b) weep   (c) three

Teeny-Tiny – 1

Read the fairy tale.

Once upon a time in a teeny-tiny village in a teeny-tiny house, there lived a teeny-tiny woman.

One day, the teeny-tiny woman put on her teeny-tiny bonnet to go for a teeny-tiny walk. After a teeny-tiny while, the teeny-tiny woman came to a teeny-tiny gate. The teeny-tiny woman opened the teeny-tiny gate. She went into a teeny-tiny graveyard. The teeny-tiny woman saw a teeny-tiny grave. On the teeny-tiny grave, the teeny-tiny woman saw a teeny-tiny bone.

'This will make some teeny-tiny soup for my teeny-tiny supper', she said. She picked up the teeny-tiny bone and put it in her teeny-tiny pocket and went home.

When the teeny-tiny woman had been asleep for a teeny-tiny time, a teeny-tiny voice spoke from the teeny-tiny cupboard.

'Give me my bone!' it said.

The teeny-tiny woman was scared. She hid her teeny-tiny head under the teeny-tiny blankets and went to sleep. After a teeny-tiny time, the teeny-tiny woman heard the teeny-tiny voice again.

'Give me my bone!' it said in a louder voice.

The teeny-tiny woman hid under the teeny-tiny blankets and went to sleep. After a teeny-tiny time, the teeny-tiny voice in the teeny-tiny cupboard spoke again.

'Give me my bone!' it said in a much louder voice.

The teeny-tiny woman put her head out of the teeny-tiny blankets and said in her loudest teeny-tiny voice, 'TAKE IT!'

My learning log	When I read this fairy tale, I could read:	☐ all of it.	☐ most of it.	☐ parts of it.

Teeny-Tiny – 2

1. What is the title of the text? _____

2. Why is this title used?

   _____

   _____

   _____

3. What words start the fairy tale?

   _____

4. Which words tell the size of all the things in the text?

   _____

5. Which word means:

   (a) 'hard pieces that make up a skeleton'? _____

   (b) 'a burial place near a church'?   _____

6. Who owns the bone?

   _____

7. What will happen to the bone after the teeny-tiny woman gives it back?

   _____

8. Where were the teeny-tiny blankets?

   _____

9. Write the name of another scary story you have heard.

   _____

10. What is found in a cupboard?

   _____

My learning log	While doing these activities:		
	I found Q _____ easy.	I found Q _____ tricky.	I found Q _____ fun.

Teeny-Tiny – 3

1. What ending is added to 'loud'?

   (a) louder _____   (b) loudest _____

2. Add '-er' and '-est' to make new adjectives.

   (a) slow   _____   _____

   (b) quiet   _____   _____

   (c) fast   _____   _____

   (d) young   _____   _____

   (e) old   _____   _____

3. Write two small words that make the compound word 'graveyard'.

   _____   _____

4. Make new compound words.

   (a) light + house   _____

   (b) bed + room   _____

   (c) basket + ball   _____

   (d) gold + fish   _____

   (e) black + berry   _____

5. The word 'teeny' has 'ee'. Fill in 'ee' and then read each word.

   (a) gr_____n   (b) m_____t   (c) w_____k   (d) tr_____

6. Follow the instructions. Write the word. Read the word.

   (a) Change the 'n' in 'green' to 't'. _____

   (b) Change the 'k' in 'week' to 'p'. _____

   (c) Change the 't' in 'tree' to 'th'. _____

My learning log	Colour:	I can add '-er' and '-est' onto words.	yes / no
		I know what a compound word is.	yes / no
		I can read 'meet', 'tree', 'week' and 'green'.	yes / no

The Child in the Loft

Teacher Information

Curriculum Links

Activity	Code	Objective	Outcome
Text	C1	• Listen to and discuss a wide range of poems at a level beyond that at which they can read independently	• Can read and discuss a poem
	C2	• Be encouraged to link what they read or hear read to their own experiences	• Can relate poem to own experiences
	C5	• Learn to appreciate rhymes and poems, and to recite some by heart	• Can identify rhyming words in poems
Comprehension	C9	• Discuss the significance of the title and events	• Can state an opinion about the title
	C10	• Make inferences on the basis of what is being said and done	• Can infer from the poem
	C11	• Predict what might happen on the basis of what has been read so far	• Can use the poem to predict events
Word Reading	WR2	• Respond speedily with the correct sound to graphemes	• Can read words with 'ue' like 'clue'
	WR3	• Read accurately by blending sounds in unfamiliar words containing GPCs that have been taught	• Can read words with 'air' like 'chair'
	WR4	• Read common exception words, noting unusual correspondences between spelling and sound and where these occur in the word	• Can read and spell common exception words such as 'your' and 'once'

Additional Teacher Information

Definition of Terms

Title
The name of a book, composition or other artistic work.

Poem
A piece of writing in which the expression of feelings and ideas is given intensity by particular attention to diction (sometimes involving rhyme), rhythm and imagery.

Links to other Curriculum Areas

• History – Changes in Living memory; common words and phrases relating to the passing of time

Terminology for Pupils

poem
word
phrase
rhyme
title

Suggested Reading

• *Me and My Family Tree* by Joan Sweeney
• *Long Ago and Today* by Rozanne Lanczak Williams
• *Life at Home (Then and Now)* by Vicki Yates

32 • • • • • • • • *Reading – Comprehension and Word Reading* • • • • • • • • • • •Prim-Ed Publishing • • • www.prim-ed.com

Text

Teacher Information

- This poem will relate to the pupils' prior experience of a wet, rainy afternoon and how they could pass the day.

Introduction

- Have a class discussion on what they do on a wet and miserable day. Ask them to think of a number of activities that they could do to enjoy their day. Ask them to think beyond computer games. Tell them that in this poem, the child in the poem found something very interesting when they had to think of something to do on a day like that.

Development

- Read and discuss the poem with the pupils. Assist them with any unfamiliar words, such as 'bonnet'. Question pupils to gauge their understanding of what they have listened to or read.
- While reading, observe and listen to see how pupils use phonic skills and knowledge to decode words.
- Assist pupils to decode more difficult words.
- If reading the poem together as a class, correct inaccurate reading.
- After reading, ask the class if they know who the child in the photo is.
- Discuss relatives in a family: great-grandmother, etc.

Differentiated Individual/Paired/Group Work

- Pupils will need different coloured pencils for this activity. Ask the pupils to reread the poem. Ask them to colour each rhyming pair of words in the same colour. In pairs, ask the pupils to think of two other rhyming words to add to each of their coloured pairs.
- Ask highly able readers to write a short paragraph telling what activities they get up to when it is a rainy afternoon. Less able readers could write short sentences, giving them a sentence starter: 'When it is a rainy afternoon, I like to …'

Review

- Pupils should share their list of rhyming words with the class. The teacher can act as a scribe and can build up a large list of rhyming words, taking contributions from each pupil pair.

Comprehension

Teacher Information

- Care may have to be taken when discussing family members. Each teacher will have to use their own discretion in this regard.

Introduction

- Reread the poem with the class. Have a quick discussion about the poem.

Development

- Discuss the comprehension activities on page 36, then allow pupils to complete the page independently.
- Compare their answers to questions that may have varied answers, especially questions 6, 7 and 8.

Differentiated Individual/Paired/Group Work

- The pupils should work in pairs and choose five words from the poem. They must work together to come up with clues that they can ask to other pairs in the class to work out which words they have chosen.
- Ask pupils to think about what they would put in their own treasure box, if they had one. Ask them to write a list and then illustrate this by drawing the treasure box.
- Ask highly able readers to think about what a child in the future would think about the things in their treasure box. Ask them to write one line predicting if the future child would be impressed or confused by any of their items.

Review

- Bring the class together and have each pair call out their clues for the words selected. Discuss the suitability of the clues they used to help identify a word.

Word Reading

Teacher Information

- The activities on page 37 focus on common exception words, words with 'ue' like 'clue' and words with 'air' like 'chair'.

Introduction

- Reread the text with the class, but first explain that the focus will be on words. While reading, ask pupils to underline the words 'clue' and 'hair'.

Development

- When they have reread the poem, ask the pupils to attempt question 1 independently. They can search for the common exception words in the poem. This question can be corrected before teaching the sounds that are targeted on this activity page.

- Remind pupils to find the word 'clue'. Discuss this word and highlight the 'ue' part. Discuss the sound that these two letters make. Can the pupils think of any words that they think have the same sound? Some pupils may think of words that have 'ew' (e.g. blew). A list can be made on the board of the different ways to write this sound. Explain to the class that they are going to focus on words that have 'ue' in them. Ask them to attempt questions 2 and 3 independently.

- Questions 4 and 5 focus on 'air' in words such as 'chair'. Ask pupils to find the sentence in the poem with the word 'hair'. Ask them to sound out the word without the 'h'. Discuss words that can be built from 'air'. Ask the pupils to suggest any that they can think of. Ask pupils to complete questions 4 and 5 independently. Ensure that pupils can read each of the words correctly.

Differentiated Individual/Paired/Group Work

- Ask highly able readers to put the words in question 2 and question 4 into their own sentences. Challenge them to see if they can make sentences containing both a 'ue' word and an 'air' word (e.g. The blue chair is in the sitting room.)

- The teacher may need to work intensively with less able readers, particularly on words that have 'ue' in them. Ensure that these pupils can sound out the words in question 2. Provide as much practice as possible to enable the pupils to master these words. Write them out on mini-flashcards and ask them to read each word and cover it over when they can read it.

Review

- Bring the class together and ensure that they can all read some selected 'ue' and 'air' words.

Assessment

C2	Ask pupils to tell you about what the poem 'The Child in the Loft' reminded them of when they heard it the first time. Ask them what they would put in their own treasure box and why.
	Record how well they were able to relate the theme of the poem to things in their own lives.
WR3	Present the following words to pupils and ask them to read them. Note the words that they struggle with and if they apply phonic knowledge and skills to decode the words:
	chair, clue, stairs, repair, glue, fuel, fairy, true, fair, value
WR4	Present the following words from the poem in isolation and record if the pupil can read them:
	said, once, weird, your, being

Answers

Comprehension

1. Answers will vary.
2. All words and phrases (yesterday, pass away the day, old, ages, faded) should be circled.
3. (a) day   (b) hid   (c) hated   (d) red
4. photographs
5. The child had red hair and freckles.
6. It was raining and the child could not go out to play.
7. Yes—There is a child playing in the loft and a child in the photograph.
8. Answers may include: The child will show it to the mother./ The child may put the book of photographs back in the box.

Word Reading

1. your/1, the/13, a/8, once/1, me/1
2. (a) blue   (b) true   (c) Tuesday   (d) rescue
       (e) tissue   (f) argue   (g) continue
3. (a) Tuesday   (b) blue   (c) tissue   (d) argue
4. (a) chair   (b) unfair   (c) airport   (d) lair
5. air, pair, repair; air, stair, stairs; air, fair, fairy, dairy

The Child in the Loft – 1

Read the poem.

Yesterday the rain fell down in sheets,

Soaking the garden, the house and the streets.

Restless and bored, with no outside play

I climbed to the loft to pass away the day.

I looked all around and what did I spy?

An old wooden box, about one foot high.

Being a curious, nosy sort, I lifted the lid

And looked inside to see what it hid.

Surely a wonderful treasure awaited

Not spiders and cobwebs — the things that I hated!

A funny old hat and clothes so weird

And a book full of photographs appeared.

I opened the book and flipped through the pages

To look at the pictures faded with the ages.

A child in a bonnet, a coat, stockings and shoes

Stared at me, but the face, so like mine, gave me a clue.

I remembered something my mother had once said.

Your great-grandmother had freckles and curly hair that was red!

My learning log	When I read this poem, I could read:	☐ all of it. ☐ most of it. ☐ parts of it.

The Child in the Loft – 2

1. Tick the people you have seen in old photographs.

    mother ☐   father ☐   grandmother ☐

    grandfather ☐   uncle ☐   aunty ☐

    great-grandmother ☐   great-grandfather ☐

2. Circle the words and phrases that tell about the passing of time.

    yesterday   pass away the day   old   ages   faded

3. Copy a word from the poem that rhymes with each word below.

    (a) play   _____   (b) lid   _____

    (c) awaited   _____   (d) said   _____

4. The word 'pictures' means the same as the word …

    _____.

5. What did the person playing in the loft look like?

    _____

    _____

6. Why was the child playing in the loft?

    _____

7. Is the title a good one? [Yes] [No] Why?

    _____

8. What do you think the child will do with the book of photographs?

    _____

My learning log	While doing these activities:		
	I found Q _____ easy.	I found Q _____ tricky.	I found Q _____ fun.

The Child in the Loft – 3

1. How many times are these words found in the poem?

   your ⬚   the ⬚   a ⬚   once ⬚   me ⬚

2. Write new words with 'ue' like 'clue'. Then read the words.

   (a) bl_____   (b) tr_____   (c) T_____sday

   (d) resc_____   (e) tiss_____   (f) arg_____   (g) contin_____

3. Use the words in question 2 to help you fill in the missing 'ue' words.

   (a) _____ always comes after Monday.

   (b) My favourite colour is _____.

   (c) I sneezed so I needed a _____.

   (d) There is no need to _____ with each other over the money.

4. Write more 'air' words like 'hair'.

   (a) ch_____   (b) unf_____   (c) _____port   (d) l_____

5. Follow the instructions to make the 'air' words.

Start with 'air'.		Start with 'air'.	
Add 'p' to the start.		Add 'st' to the start.	
Add 're' to the start.		Add 's' to the end.	
The new word is:		The new word is:	

Start with 'air'.	
Add 'f' to the start.	
Add 'y' to the end.	
Change 'f' to 'd'.	
The new word is:	

My learning log	*Colour:*	I can read 'once', 'your' and 'the'.	yes / no
		I know the sound 'ue' makes so I can read 'blue', 'argue' and 'tissue'.	yes / no
		I can read words like 'chair', 'lair' and 'repair'.	yes / no

Read the folk tale.

One day, Henny Penny was picking up corn in the cornfield when something hit her on the head.

'The sky is falling', said Henny Penny. 'I must go and tell the king.'

On the way, she met Cocky Locky.

'I am going to tell the king the sky is falling', said Henny Penny. Cocky Locky wanted to go too. So off they went to see the king.

Henny Penny and Cocky Locky met Ducky Daddles. Ducky Daddles wanted to go to tell the king too. So off they went.

Henny Penny, Cocky Locky and Ducky Daddles met Goosey Poosey. Goosey Poosey wanted to go to tell the king too. So off they went.

Henny Penny, Cocky Locky, Ducky Daddles and Goosey Poosey met Turkey Lurkey. Turkey Lurkey wanted to go to tell the king too. So off they went.

Henny Penny, Cocky Locky, Ducky Daddles, Goosey Poosey and Turkey Lurkey met Foxy Woxy.

'I will take you to the king', he said. So all the animals followed Foxy Woxy to tell the king the sky was falling.

He took them to his cave. The animals went in one by one. Foxy Woxy snapped off the head of each one. He threw their bodies in a pile. Henny Penny heard Cocky Locky cry out. She ran away back to her home.

She never told the king that the sky was falling.

Name: _____ Class: _____ Date: _____

Henny Penny

1. What fell on Henny Penny's head? Tick one or more.

   ☐ the sky   ☐ an acorn   ☐ an apple   ☐ a lorry

   1 mark

2. Write a number from 1 to 5 to show the order of the animals in the story.

   Turkey Lurkey ☐   Henny Penny ☐

   Goosey Poosey ☐   Ducky Daddles ☐

   Cocky Locky ☐

   1 mark

3. Why did Henny Penny want to tell the king that the sky was falling?

   _____

   _____

   2 marks

4. Which event stopped the animals from seeing the king?

   _____

   _____

   1 mark

5. What do you think Henny Penny will do next time something hits her on the head? Tick one.

   ☐ She will go to tell the king.

   ☐ She will tell her animal friends.

   ☐ She will ignore it.

   1 mark

Total for this page	/6

Henny Penny

1. Tick the word that does not have two syllables.

☐ something

☐ wanted

☐ followed

☐ pile

2. Circle 'one' or 'more than one' for each noun.

(a) king | one | more than one |

(b) animals | one | more than one |

3. What ending has been added to each verb?

(a) falling   _____

(b) wanted   _____

(c) picking   _____

(d) followed _____

4. Which verb is the correct one to use? Tick one.

(a) Foxes *eat* other animals.   ☐

(b) Foxes *eats* other animals.   ☐

| Total for this page | /4 | Total for this assessment | /10 |

Henny Penny

Genre: Folk tale

Breakdown of question type/content and mark allocation

Comprehension		Word Reading	
Q 1. Inferring	1 mark	**Q 1.** Syllables	1 mark
Q 2. Sequencing	1 mark	**Q 2.** Singular and plural	1 mark
Q 3. Inferring	2 marks	**Q 3.** Suffixes '-ing' and '-ed'	1 mark
Q 4. Finding information	1 mark	**Q 4.** Verbs	1 mark
Q 5. Predicting	1 mark		
Sub-total		Sub-total	
		Record the pupil's total result for this assessment.	

Assessment – Henny Penny

Comprehension .... *Page 39*

1. 'an acorn' and 'an apple' may be ticked
2. Henny Penny 1,
   Cocky Locky 2,
   Ducky Daddles 3,
   Goosey Poosey 4,
   Turkey Lurkey 5
3. Henny Penny thought the king could stop the sky from falling; Henny Penny thought the king was so powerful he could fix anything—even stop the sky from falling.
4. Foxy Loxy tricked the animals into going into his cave and then he ate them.
5. She will ignore it.

Word Reading .... *Page 40*

1. pile
2. (a) one   (b) more than one
3. (a) -ing   (b) -ed   (c) -ing   (d) -ed
4. (a) Foxes eat other animals.

Lizzy Lizard's Adventure

Curriculum Links

Activity	Code	Objective	Outcome
Text	C1 C5	• Listen to and discuss a wide range of poems at a level beyond that at which they can read independently • Learn to appreciate rhymes and poems, and to recite some by heart	• Can read a poem • Can recognise pairs of rhyming words
Comprehension	C2 C6 C7	• Be encouraged to link what they read or hear read to their own experiences • Discuss word meanings, linking new meanings to those already known • Draw on what they already know or on background information provided by the teacher	• Can relate to being in a big city • Can define words from the poem • Can tell what they know about lizards
Word Reading	WR1 WR3	• Apply phonic knowledge and skills as the route to decode words • Read accurately by blending sounds in unfamiliar words	• Can read words that contain 'll' and 'zz' • Can read 'ai' words

Additional Teacher Information

Definition of Terms

Poem
A piece of writing in which the expression of feelings and ideas is given intensity by particular attention to diction (sometimes involving rhyme), rhythm and imagery.

Links to other Curriculum Areas

• Geography:
Locational knowledge: name, locate and identify the four countries and capital cities of the United Kingdom
Human and physical geography: use basic geographical vocabulary to refer to
   – key physical features—sea, river, bay, hill, ridge
   – key human features—port, bridge, castle, fort, city, country
Geographical skills and fieldwork: use simple compass directions—near, far, north, south, back

• Science – Animals, including humans (Identify and name a variety of common animals including reptiles; Identify and name a variety of common animals that are carnivores)

Terminology for Pupils

poem
word
rhyme

Suggested Reading

• *The Ant Explorer* by C J Dennis
• *You Clumsy Gray Lizard* by Margo Fallis at <http://www.electricscotland.com/kids/stories/logan.htm>
• *Usborne Sticker Atlas of Britain and Northern Ireland* by Stephanie Turnbull
• *A Lizard Got into the Paint Pots* by Jill Pickering
• *Emma's Strange Pet* by Jean Little

Text

Teacher Information

- This poem tells the story of Lizzy Lizard as she travels around the United Kingdom. The place names London, Edinburgh, Belfast and Cardiff are mentioned.

Introduction

- Discuss the cities of London, Edinburgh, Belfast and Cardiff. Have the pupils heard of all of them? Have any of them visited these cities? Use a map to show where each of the places are.

Development

- Read and discuss the text with the pupils. The text includes the names of the capital cities of the four countries that make up the United Kingdom. Assist them with any unfamiliar words such as 'roam', 'travel', 'trails', 'ridges', 'fort', 'port', 'bay', 'dreary', 'weary', 'thrills', 'decided' and 'country'. Question pupils to gauge their understanding of what they have listened to or read.

- While reading, observe to see how pupils use phonic skills and knowledge to decode words. Assist pupils to decode more difficult words.

- If reading the poem together as a class, correct inaccurate reading.

- Teachers should identify any words containing any sounds or word patterns relevant to their teaching activities. For example, 'ear' in 'dreary' and 'weary'; 'ff' in 'Cardiff', 'll' in 'hills' and 'thrills' and so on.

- Teachers may wish to refer to a map of the United Kingdom during or after reading the poem.

Differentiated Individual/Paired/Group Work

- In pairs, have pupils make a list of all the things that Lizzie saw on her trip. They can then organise these words. Use the four cities as headings, and place the things under the correct city.

- More able readers could write sentences, using the structure 'In _____, Lizzy Lizard saw ...'

Review

- Have the class perform a group reading of the poem. Assign two rhyming lines to each group and have them read the poem in the correct order. Careful listening will be required to read the poem correctly.

Comprehension

Teacher Information

- This poem tells the story of Lizzy Lizard as she travels around the United Kingdom. The place names London, Edinburgh, Belfast and Cardiff are mentioned.

Introduction

- Discuss the poem with the pupils. Can they remember where Lizzy went? Can they remember any of the things that she saw while on her travels? Reread the poem with the pupils.

Development

- Discuss the comprehension activities on page 46, then allow pupils to complete the page independently.

- Compare their answers to questions that may have varied answers, especially questions 1, 4 and 5.

Differentiated Individual/Paired/Group Work

- Highly able pupils should write about a city they have visited. Where did they go? Where did they stay? Who went with them? What did they see? What was the best thing they did there? Highly able readers can write two paragraphs; less able readers can discuss the topic with the teacher and write a few sentences about their experience.

Review

- Select a few volunteers to briefly read out their paragraph or sentences.

Word Reading

Teacher Information

- The activities on page 47 focus on words containing 'll' and 'zz', rhyming words and words with 'ai', such as 'snail'.

Introduction

- Reread the text with the class, but first explain that the focus will be on words. While reading, ask pupils to find rhyming words for 'dreary' ('weary') and 'clocks' ('docks').

Development

- Discuss with the pupils the rhyming words they identified while reading the text. Talk about the pairs of rhyming words. Ask them if they know of any other words that can be used in the same rhyming group.

- Focus on the word 'snail'. Ask the pupils to identify the 'ai' sound when you say it. Can they correctly identify the two letters used to represent this sound? Using their knowledge of rhyming words, ask them to suggest other words that have that sound in them. Make a list on the board. (Any words that are suggested that have the same sound but are spelt with different graphemes can be written in a second list on the board.) Explain that today's focus is on 'ai' words.

- Discuss the word reading activities on page 47, then allow pupils to complete the page independently.

Differentiated Individual/Paired/Group Work

- Have highly able readers work in pairs to write a simple poem using sets of rhyming words.

- Work with less able readers on the 'ai' sound. Help them read and write these words. Ask them to orally put these words in sentences. Act as a scribe and write out the sentences they think of but have them write the target 'ai' word into the sentences. After all sentences have been written, have the pupils read out all the sentences.

Review

- Bring the whole class together and ask selected pairs to read out the poems they have written.

- Finish off with a word game. Say a word from the poem and ask the pupils what the rhyming word in the poem was.

Assessment

C5	Ask pupils to individually do a rhyming task with you. Present the following words from the poem and ask the pupil to tell you the rhyming word. As an extra challenge, ask highly able readers to suggest an extra rhyming word not in the text of the poem.
	port, trails, dizzy, hills, home
C6	Ask the pupils to write the following words in a simple sentence that shows the meaning:
	castle, weary, travel, floating, docks
WR1	Ask pupils to fill in the missing letters to spell the following 'ai' words. Clues are provided.
	_ _ail (animal) _ain (falls from sky) _ _ain (type of transport) _ _raid (scared) _ai_ (used with a hammer) _ai_ (a fox and dog have one)

Answers

Comprehension

1. Teacher check
2. (a) fort (b) insect (c) cliff (d) dock
3. north, south
4. Lizzy was tired of roaming and wanted to go home.
5. Lizzy was weary of new things and places.
6. (a) be (b) dizzy (c) fort (d) home
7. Teacher check
8. Teacher check

Word Reading

1. Lizzy, dizzy
2. all, travelled, thrills, hills, I'll
3. home/roam, bridges/ridges, port/fort, hills/thrills, snails/trails, sea/be
4. hills = red, port = blue, snails = green, bridges = yellow
5. (a) snail (b) trail (c) rain
   (d) train (e) paid (f) afraid
6. (a) snail, train (b) rain (c) afraid

Lizzy Lizard's Adventure – 1

Read the poem.

Once a little lizard made up her mind to roam

To travel here, to travel there, far away from home.

She had eaten all her insects, her worms and all her snails.

Her mother said it was okay, so Lizzy started along the trails.

She left London where the river flowed underneath the bridges

And travelled north to Edinburgh to see castles on high ridges.

She moved around the northern islands floating in the sea.

To the south, she came to Belfast, on a river as blue as can be.

In Cardiff, she saw a river, a bay and a fort

And crawled among the ships visiting the port.

She saw the docks, the castles and some hills,

But Lizzy soon began to grow tired of the thrills.

A dreary lizard, a weary lizard decided no more to roam.

She travelled back through all the cities until she reached her home.

'I didn't know this country was so big', said Lizzy,

'I think I'll stay under my rock. Other places make me dizzy!'

My learning log	When I read this poem, I could read:	☐ all of it. ☐ most of it. ☐ parts of it.

Lizzy Lizard's Adventure – 2

1. Write something you know about lizards.

_____

_____

2. Match each word to its meaning.

(a) a strong place used to protect a place   •   •   insect

(b) a small animal with six legs and wings   •   •   fort

(c) a steep rock face near the sea   •   •   dock

(d) a place for loading and unloading ships   •   •   cliff

3. Write two words that tell about directions on a map.

_____   _____

4. Why did Lizzy decide to go back home? _____

_____

5. Why was Lizzy weary? _____

_____

6. Which word rhymes with:

(a) sea? _____   (b) Lizzy? _____

(c) port? _____   (d) roam? _____

7. Do you think Lizzy will go on a long

journey again? [Yes] [No]

8. Write the name of any city in the poem you have visited.

_____

My learning log	While doing these activities:		
	I found Q _____ easy.	I found Q _____ tricky.	I found Q _____ fun.

Lizzy Lizard's Adventure – 3

1. Write two words from the poem that have 'zz'.

   _____   _____

2. Write two words from the poem that have 'll'.

   _____   _____

3. Find and write the rhyming words from the poem.

home	bridges	port
hills	snails	sea

4. Look at all the words in question 3. Follow the instructions.

The box that has the same word family as 'bills'. Colour that box red.	The box that has the same word family as 'sort'. Colour that box blue.
The box that has the same word family as 'emails'. Colour that box green.	The box that has the same word family as 'fridges'. Colour that box yellow.

5. Write 'ai' into these words and read them.

   (a) sn_____l   (b) tr_____l   (c) r_____n

   (d) tr_____n   (e) p_____d   (f) afr_____d

6. Fill in the missing words. Use the words from question 5 to help you.

   (a) A _____ is much slower than a _____.

   (b) The _____ made my clothes wet.

   (c) The kitten was _____ of the big dog.

My learning log	Colour:	I know what a rhyming word is.	yes / no
		I can read 'rain', 'paid' and 'snail'.	yes / no

Curriculum Links

Activity	Code	Objective	Outcome
Text	C1	• Listen to and discuss a wide range of non-fiction at a level beyond that at which they can read independently	• Can read and discuss a recipe
	C7	• Draw on what they already know or on background information and vocabulary provided by the teacher	• Can follow instructions
Comprehension	C8	• Check that the text makes sense to them as they read and correct inaccurate reading	• Can understand the steps of a recipe
	C13	• Explain clearly their understanding of what is read to them	
Word Reading	WR4	• Read common exception words, noting unusual correspondences between spelling and sound and where these occur in the word	• Can make plurals of words with -s and -es endings
	WR5	• Read words containing taught GPCs and -s and -es endings	

Additional Teacher Information

Definition of Terms

Recipe

A recipe is a procedure or set of instructions for preparing a particular dish, including a list of the ingredients required. A procedure tells how to make or do something. It uses clear, concise language and command verbs. A recipe is an informational text.

Terminology for Pupils

recipe
instruction/step
word
bracket
compound word
double letters

Links to other Curriculum Areas

• Personal, social, health and economic education (PSHE) – Diet for a healthy lifestyle
• Mathematics – Measurement (measuring mass/weight and capacity in grams and millilitres)

Suggested Reading

• *Once Upon a Time in the Kitchen: Recipes and Tales from Classic Children's Stories (Myths, Legends, Fairy and Folk Tales)* by Carol Odell (stories for listening)
• *Fancy Nancy: Tea Parties* by Jane O'Connor
• *Tyler Makes a Birthday Cake! (Tyler and Tofu)* by Tyler Florence
• *Tiny Pie* by Mark Bailey

Text

Teacher Information

- This English dessert is traditionally served at the annual cricket game between Eton College and Harrow School.
- The three main ingredients are strawberries, cream and meringue. Some people believe the dessert got its name because a meringue dessert was accidentally crushed by a dog while in transit to a picnic at Eton. It was served as a 'messy' dessert of crushed meringues, cream and strawberries.

Introduction

- Have a discussion with pupils about desserts. Ask pupils if they know the names of some of the more popular desserts. Ask pupils when desserts are served. Ask them what desserts usually have as ingredients. Explain that they will read a recipe to make a dessert. Ask pupils where they might find a recipe. Discuss the name of the dessert. Does the word 'mess' sound good or bad in a recipe?

Development

- Read and discuss the text with the pupils. Assist them with any unfamiliar words such as units of measure, or the list of ingredients. One tricky word in this text is 'meringue'. Explain that this word is a French word that we now use in English. Point out the tricky ending for the pupils. Explain what the 'Steps' mean. Question pupils to gauge their understanding of what they have listened to or read.
- While reading, observe and listen to see how pupils use phonic skills and knowledge to decode words. Assist pupils to decode more difficult words.
- If reading the recipe together as a class, correct inaccurate reading.
- Teachers may need to pronounce some words and exaggerate the sound being identified to assist pupils to answer any questions relating to phonic skills and knowledge.
- Ask the pupils to work together to explain how to make Eton Mess.

Differentiated Individual/Paired/Group Work

- Ask pupils to work in pairs and to list the ingredients and then to illustrate each step of the recipe.
- Allow highly able readers to research their favourite dessert and to make a list of the ingredients that would be needed to create it.
- The teacher could work with a small group of less able readers to look at all the compound words in the recipe (this is the focus of the word reading activities, so practice at this point would ensure higher confidence to answer these questions in a later lesson).

Review

- Summarise the main features of the recipe.

Comprehension

Teacher Information

- This English dessert is traditionally served at the annual cricket game between Eton College and Harrow School.
- The three main ingredients are strawberries, cream and meringue. Some people believe the dessert got its name because a meringue dessert was accidentally crushed by a dog while in transit to a picnic at Eton. It was served as a 'messy' dessert of crushed meringues, cream and strawberries.

Introduction

- Pupils take it in turns to retell how to make Eton Mess. They must list all the ingredients first, then outline the steps to make it.

Development

- Discuss the comprehension activities on page 52, then allow the pupils to complete the page independently.
- Question 8 will have very different answers, so this can lead to a discussion.

Differentiated Individual/Paired/Group Work

- Have pupils work in pairs to write a recipe for their favourite sandwich. Encourage them to follow the recipe layout and to use the Eton Mess recipe as a template (stating how many it will serve, the list of ingredients and the steps).
- With adult support, have groups work to create this dessert. They must be encouraged to read out each step clearly and follow the instructions. Discuss issues such as hygiene and safe food preparation. (Alternatively, do this as a whole class activity and ask groups to perform different steps in the recipe.)

Review

- Have pupils read out their recipes for creating their favourite sandwich.

Word Reading

Teacher Information

- The activities on page 53 focus on the singular and plural of nouns, compound words and double letters in words.

Introduction

- Reread the text, but first explain to the pupils that the focus will be on words. While reading, ask the pupils to underline all the plural words they see.

Development

- After reading, ask the pupils to share the plural words they found in the recipe. Write a list on the board. Divide into three columns. Ask pupils to come up with the rules for making the plural: most words add '-s', but some words add '-es' (discuss if they can see a rule for adding '-es'). One of the columns will have plurals made from words ending in '-y'. Even though this is not the focus of this lesson, draw pupils' attention to this feature (berry; berries).

- Discuss compound words. This concept has been introduced in Unit 5, but this unit may not have been covered yet. Introduce the term compound words. Use some of the words in the text, 'tablespoon' and 'strawberry', to demonstrate that the two words are separate and have separate meanings. When combined they take on a different meaning. Use other common examples such as 'butterfly', 'armchair', 'lipstick', 'cupcake' and 'cartwheel'.

- Discuss the word reading activities on page 53, then allow pupils to complete the page independently.

Differentiated Individual/Paired/Group Work

- Ask pupils to draw pictures of the compound words: their individual words and the word created when they are joined.

- Ask highly able readers to write out the recipe but this time change some of the steps slightly. They can then give their wrong steps to a partner who has to read the steps and correct any mistakes.

Review

- As a whole class, ask pupils to think of more compound words (not mentioned in the recipe). If possible, the pupils can give clues to the compound word they are thinking of.

Assessment

C13	Have pupils orally recount how they would make Eton Mess. See if they use the vocabulary associated with a recipe (e.g. ingredients, steps, fold, beat, chill).
	Note as part of the assessment how methodical the pupil is in outlining the steps involved in the recipe. Does he/she miss out any steps? Does he/she explain clearly?
WR4	Present two lists of words and ask pupils to join them to make compound words.

List 1	List 2
sun	bow
rain	fighter
fire	bird
lady	flower

Answers

Comprehension

1. Answers will vary.
2. (a) blue/purple   (b) black/dark purple
3. All should be ticked.
4. grams, tablespoon, teaspoon, mL
5. mixed berries, icing sugar, double cream, vanilla extract, Greek yoghurt, meringue nests
6. cream
7. Answers may include lemon meringue pie, baked Alaska, pavlova etc.
8. Answers will vary.

Word Reading

1. (a) one   (b) more than more
2. (a) dishes (b) brushes (c) boxes (d) buses
3. (a) foxes   (b) classes   (c) mosses
   (d) bushes   (e) lashes
4. (a) blue, berry   (b) black, berry   (c) straw, berry
   (d) tea, spoon   (e) table, spoon
5. Teacher check

Eton Mess – 1

Read the recipe.

Follow the instructions to make a yummy dessert called Eton Mess.

Serves four people

You will need:

- 260 grams mixed berries (blueberries, blackberries, strawberries or raspberries)

- 1 tablespoon icing sugar plus 1 teaspoon extra

- 125 mL double cream

- quarter teaspoon vanilla extract

- 1 x 200 gram pot Greek yoghurt

- 2 meringue nests, broken into pieces

- mixer and bowl

- spoon

- large bowl

- small bowls or glasses

Steps:

1. Put berries into large bowl. Add tablespoon icing sugar and mix lightly.

2. Put cream, 1 teaspoon icing sugar and vanilla extract in mixer bowl and whip until soft peaks form.

3. Fold yoghurt into cream, then berries and meringue.

4. Spoon into small bowls or glasses. Chill for a few minutes.

5. Eat and enjoy!

How did you do?

Do you think you could make this? Do you think it will taste yummy?

My learning log	When I read this recipe, I could read:	☐ all of it. ☐ most of it. ☐ parts of it.

Eton Mess – 2

1. Tick the berries you have eaten.

   blueberries ☐   blackberries ☐

   strawberries ☐   raspberries ☐

2. What colour are:

   (a) blueberries? _____

   (b) blackberries? _____

3. Tick the parts of a recipe.

   (a) a list of things you need   ☐   (b) steps ☐

   (c) the name of the thing you are making   ☐

4. Write four words that are units of measure.

   _____

5. Write six ingredients you need to make Eton Mess.

   _____

   _____

6. Which word means 'fatty liquid on the top of milk'?

   _____

7. What other dessert is made with meringue?

   _____

8. Do you think you will enjoy eating this dessert? ☐ Yes ☐ No

   Why? _____

   _____

My learning log	While doing these activities:		
	I found Q _____ easy.	I found Q _____ tricky.	I found Q _____ fun.

Eton Mess – 3

1. How many? One or more than one?

    (a) glass | one | | more than one |

    (b) glasses | one | | more than one |

2. Add '-es' to make the words say more than one.

    (a) dish _____

    (b) brush _____

    (c) box _____

    (d) bus _____

3. Change each word in brackets to make it correct.

    (a) Three (fox) _____ came near the henhouse.

    (b) The two Year 1 (class) _____ went on a trip.

    (c) The forest was full of (moss) _____ .

    (d) The gardener planted (bush) _____ all around the garden.

    (e) My eye (lash) _____ keep my eyes safe from dust.

4. Which two words make each compound word?

    (a) blueberry _____ _____

    (b) blackberry _____ _____

    (c) strawberry _____ _____

    (d) teaspoon _____ _____

    (e) tablespoon _____ _____

5. Draw a line under the double letters.

    | mess   vanilla   berries   glasses   chill   small |

My learning log	*Colour:*	I can make the plural of 'glass', 'bowl' and 'box'.	yes / no
		I know what a compound word is.	yes / no
		I can give three examples of compound words.	yes / no

Hedgehogs

Curriculum Links

Activity	Code	Objective	Outcome
Text	C1 C6	• Listen to and discuss a wide range of non-fiction at a level beyond that at which they can read independently • Discuss word meanings, linking new meanings to those already known	• Can read a report • Can discuss the meanings of words such as 'nocturnal', 'omnivores' and 'hibernate'
Comprehension	C12 C13	• Participate in discussion about what is read to them, taking turns and listening to what others say • Explain clearly their understanding of what is read to them	• Can tell the main points of a report • Can summarise what they have read
Word Reading	WR2 WR5 WR6	• Respond speedily with the correct sound to graphemes • Read words containing -s, -es, -er and -est endings • Read other words of more than one syllable that contain taught GPCs	• Can read words with 'au' • Can add '-er' and '-est' to words • Can read words with up to three syllables

Additional Teacher Information

Definition of Terms

Report

A report is a written document describing the findings of an individual or group. A report may take the form of a newspaper report, sports or police report, or a report about an animal, person or object.

Terminology for Pupils

report
word
syllable
adjective
sound

Links to other Curriculum Areas

• Science – Animals, including humans (Identify and name a variety of common animals including mammals; Identify and name a variety of common animals that are omnivores)

Suggested Reading

• *About Mammals: A Guide for Children (About (Peachtree))* by Cathryn Sill
• *The Tale of Mrs Tiggy-Winkle* by Beatrix Potter
• *Hedgie's Surprise* by Jan Brett
• *The Hodgeheg* by Dick King-Smith
• *Hedgehog in the Fog* by Yuri Norstein

Text

Teacher Information

- This text presents a report on hedgehogs. This provides excellent cross-curricular links with science.

Introduction

- If the class have studied animals already, use this as an opportunity to revise the topics they have learned so far. Tell the class that they are going to learn about a common mammal called the hedgehog. Ask the pupils if they have any knowledge about hedgehogs. Write any information on a chart or on the board. Tell them that they are going to read a report. Explain that this will give a lot of factual information about the hedgehog.

Development

- Read and discuss the text with the pupils. Ask questions to gauge understanding, including the vocabulary 'mammals', 'snout', 'hedges', 'spines', 'burrows', 'hollow' and 'blind'. Ensure pupils clearly understand, from the explanation given in the text, the meaning of the words 'mammal', 'nocturnal' and 'hibernate'.

- When discussing information texts, consider what the pupils may already know about the topic. Teachers may need to explain the difference in pronunciation between '... live young' and '... live in ...'.

- Question pupils to gauge their understanding of what they have listened to or read. While reading, observe to see how pupils use phonic skills and knowledge to decode words. Assist pupils to decode more difficult words.

- If reading the text together as a class, correct inaccurate reading.

Differentiated Individual/Paired/Group Work

- Working in pairs, have each partner take turns to explain the facts that they remember from the report.

- Have pupils write down five short sentences based on the facts they have learned about hedgehogs; highly able readers can write ten sentences.

- Working in groups, have the pupils make a list of all the new vocabulary. Have them devise word meaning clues. All the groups can participate in a vocabulary quiz. The teacher can keep a track of the score. Each group must ask and answer questions from other groups.

Review

- As a whole class, summarise the main points of the report.

Comprehension

Teacher Information

- When answering questions 3 and 4 on page 58, teachers should accept suitable answers from pupils who are knowledgeable about the topic.

Introduction

- Pupils take it in turns to recall the facts of the report. While they are telling the facts, the teacher can seek further clarification. For example, if the pupil uses a word from the text, the teacher should call on another pupil to explain what that word means.

Development

- Discuss the comprehension activities on page 58, then allow the pupils to complete the page independently.

- Compare their answers to questions 1 and 5, as these will have varied answers.

Differentiated Individual/Paired/Group Work

- The pupils may have already read the report in Unit 4, 'What is a Plant?'. They should be more familiar with the structure of a report. Linking with a lesson on science, pick another animal that you would like the class to study (or allow pupils to pick their favourite animal). In small groups, have pupils research the animal and find out information about its life. They can write these ideas down on pieces of paper. The sentences can be short and the teacher can provide help wherever needed. When they have all the information gathered, they can write a report on the animal. Encourage them to use pictures and illustrations. This may take a couple of lessons to complete but will integrate science effectively.

- Each group could be given some modelling clay to create a clay model of the animal. Display the results around the classroom.

Review

- Invite some groups to come up and share their progress on their report. They won't have it all finished in one lesson, but the teacher can still ask them what they intend to put in the report, what other information they have to find, where they are going to find it etc.

Word Reading

Teacher Information

- The activities on page 59 focus on synonyms, syllables, adding '-er' and '-est' to words and words with 'au'.

Introduction

- Reread the text, but this time explain to the pupils that the focus will be on the words that are used. While reading, ask the pupils to underline the following (write on the board to help pupils): the name of the hedgehog's home ('burrow'), the long sleep that hedgehogs take ('hibernate') and the plural of 'leaf' ('leaves').

Development

- Ensure pupils are familiar with syllables (they have been covered in previous units). Pick a number of words from the text and have pupils clap out the number of syllables they hear. Use words such as mammals, baby, sleep, seven, interesting, protect, animals, tail. Discuss how syllables can help pupils when reading and writing.
- Discuss words that can have '-er' and '-est' added to them. Use the following words from the report (young – younger, youngest/ strong – stronger, strongest/sharp – sharper, sharpest/stiff – stiffer, stiffest).
- Words with 'au' include 'autumn', 'author', 'dinosaur' and 'August'. Have pupils say these words. Emphasise the 'au' part. Underline it and talk about the shape our mouth makes when saying this.
- Discuss the word reading activities on page 59, then allow the pupils to complete the page independently.

Differentiated Individual/Paired/Group Work

- In pairs, pupils can be asked to do some revision work on the singular and plural of words. Ask them to find any plural words in the report and write the singular word beside the plural.
- Have highly able readers work in pairs. Ask them to pick some words they have read recently. Make a list of ten words. Write each word and draw syllable boxes beside each one. They should give this to their partner and each pupil can work on their syllable boxes. The teacher can provide assistance with any tricky words they have chosen.

Review

- As a class, pupils revise the key aspects of the lesson. Give them quick review questions. For example, How many syllables has 'autumn'?/'dinosaur'?

Assessment

C6	Present the following list of words to the pupils on the board. On the other side of the board, present a list of meanings (but in a random order). The pupils must assign the correct meaning to each word. Words: mammal, snout, nocturnal, omnivore, hibernate, protect Meanings: sleep during the day, awake at night keep safe from danger animal with hair or fur that gives birth to live young sleep during winter type of animal nose animal that eats plants and other animals
C13	Ask pupils to tell you all the things they have learned from the report on hedgehogs. Each pupil must tell at least five things they have learned.
WR5	Ask pupils to write three sentences for each of the two following sets of words: young – younger – youngest short – shorter – shortest

Answers

Comprehension

1. Answers will vary.
2. (a) nocturnal—sleep during the day; awake at night
   (b) hibernate—sleep during winter
3. Answers may include: badger, owl or mouse.
4. Answers may include: bear and squirrel.
5. It finds food in hedges and grunts like a hog/pig.
6. It wakes up and eats lots of food.
7. … has hair or fur, gives birth to live young and feeds young with own milk.
8. It rolls up into a ball to show its spines and scare the fox away.
9. piglets

Word Reading

1. (a) snout   (b) hibernate
   (c) burrow   (d) protect
2. (a) spines (one syllable)   (b) om/ni/vores
   (c) noc/tur/nal   (d) hi/ber/nate
3. (a) longer   (b) shorter
4. (a) longest   (b) shortest
5. Answers may include:
   hedgehogs, mammals, hedges, plants, toes, claws, eyes, ears, spines, themselves, animals, foxes, omnivores, insects, snails, lizards, frogs, worms, seeds, birds, eggs, burrows, nests, leaves, logs, babies, hoglets, years
6. au
7. (a) author   (b) autumn   (c) dinosaur

Hedgehogs – 1

Read the report.

Hedgehogs are mammals. Mammals have hair or fur. Mother mammals give birth to live young. They feed them with their own milk.

Hedgehogs have a long snout (nose) for digging under hedges and plants for food.

They have a short tail and five toes on each foot. They have strong claws for digging. They have large eyes and ears.

The hair on the back of a hedgehog makes sharp, stiff spines. When hedgehogs roll up into a ball to protect themselves, their spines stick up. They scare away animals like foxes.

Hedgehogs are nocturnal. They sleep during the day and are awake at night.

Hedgehogs are omnivores. They eat other animals and plants with their sharp teeth. Insects, small mice, snails, lizards, frogs, worms, seeds, fruit and birds' eggs are food for hedgehogs.

They live in burrows, nests made from leaves and grass, or hollow logs. Hedgehogs live by themselves unless they are making babies.

Baby hedgehogs are called hoglets. When they are born, they are blind and have no hair.

Hedgehogs hibernate (sleep) during winter, so they eat lots of food in autumn.

Hedgehogs grunt like a pig or hog.

Hedgehogs live for about seven years.

Hedgehogs are very interesting mammals.

My learning log	When I read this report, I could read:	☐ all of it. ☐ most of it. ☐ parts of it.

Hedgehogs – 2

1. Have you ever seen a hedgehog? ⬚ Yes ⬚ No Where?

   _____

   _____

2. Draw a line to match the words to their meanings.

   (a) nocturnal   •   •   sleep during winter

   (b) hibernate   •   •   sleep during the day; awake at night

3. What other animal is nocturnal? _____

4. What other animal hibernates? _____

5. How do you think a hedgehog got its name?

   _____

   _____

6. What happens to a hedgehog in spring?

   _____

   _____

7. Write three things that tell what a mammal is. A mammal is an

   animal that ... _____

   _____.

8. What happens when a hedgehog sees a fox?

   _____

   _____

9. Baby hedgehogs are called hoglets. Baby pigs are called ...

   _____.

My learning log	While doing these activities:		
	I found Q _____ easy.	I found Q _____ tricky.	I found Q _____ fun.

Hedgehogs – 3

1. Find words in the report that mean the same as these words.

   (a) nose _____ (b) sleep _____

   (c) hedgehog's home _____ (d) keep safe _____

2. Write each word correctly in the syllable boxes.

   (a) spines

   (b) omnivores

   (c) nocturnal

   (d) hibernate

3. Add '-er' to make new adjectives.

   (a) long _____ (b) short _____

4. Add '-est' to make new words.

   (a) long _____ (b) short _____

5. Find three words with '-s' or '-es' on the end that say more than one.

   _____

6. Circle the sound that is the same in each word.

autumn	author	dinosaur	August

7. Fill in the missing words. Use question 6 to help you.

   (a) The _____ wrote an interesting book.

   (b) There are three months in _____.

   (c) It would be amazing to find a _____ bone.

My learning log	Colour:	I can tell the syllables in *hedgehog* and *burrow*.	yes / no
		I can add '-er' and '-est' to words.	yes / no
		I can read these words *autumn*, *August* and *author*.	yes / no

The Cheeses That Ran Away

Curriculum Links

Activity	Code	Objective	Outcome
Text	C11	• Predict what might happen on the basis of what has been read so far	• Can predict from reading a folk tale
Comprehension	C3	• Become very familiar with traditional tales, retelling them and considering their particular characteristics	• Can retell the folk tale
	C8	• Check that the text makes sense to them as they read and correct inaccurate reading	• Can ask and answer questions during reading
Word Reading	WR3	• Read accurately by blending sounds in unfamiliar words containing GPCs that have been taught	• Can read words with 'ar' like 'farmer'
	WR4	• Read common exception words, noting unusual correspondences between spelling and sound and where these occur in the word	• Can read common exception words
	WR5	• Read words containing taught GPCs and -s and -es endings	• Can recognise singular and plural

Additional Teacher Information

Definition of Terms

Title
The name of a book, composition or other artistic work.

Text
A book or other written or printed work, regarded in terms of its content rather than its physical form.

Folk tale
A folk tale is a story passed from one generation to the next by word of mouth rather than being written down. A folk tale may include sayings, superstitions, social rituals, and legends or lore about the weather, animals or plants.

Links to other Curriculum Areas

• Geography – Locational knowledge (the town of Nottingham and the village of Gotham); Human and physical geography (basic geographical vocabulary including bridge, market and hill)

• Personal, social, health and economic education (PSHE) – Diet for a healthy lifestyle

Terminology for Pupils

folk tale
title
text
word
sound
sentence

Suggested Reading

• *Johnny-Cake* (traditional folk tale) (Refer to <http://www.sacred-texts.com/neu/eng//eft/eft29.htm>)

• *The Gingerbread Man* (traditional tale)

• *The Stinky Cheese Man and Other Fairly Stupid Tales* by Jon Scieszka

• *The King, the Mice and the Cheese (Beginner Books)* by Nancy Gurney

• *Where's My Cheese, Please?* by David Martin (a rhyming text)

• *From Milk to Cheese (First Facts: From Farm to Table)* by Roberta Basel

Text

Teacher Information

- This is a traditional folk tale. A number of place names are mentioned (York, Gotham and Nottingham) so a map might be useful to help pupils.

Introduction

- Tell the pupils that they are going to read a folk tale called 'The Cheeses That Ran Away'. Based on the title, ask pupils to predict what it might be about. How could cheese run away? Ask them to think in pairs about what it could be about. Discuss these ideas and see at the end if any pair was close to the idea.

Development

- Read and discuss the text with the pupils. Assist them with any unfamiliar words such as 'yourself' and 'themselves' and place names like Gotham, Nottingham and York. Some discussion may be required regarding markets and the various types possible. Question pupils to gauge their understanding of what they have listened to or read. While reading, observe to see how pupils use phonic skills and knowledge to decode words.
- Assist pupils to decode more difficult words.
- If reading the text together as a class, correct inaccurate reading.
- Teachers may wish to help pupils find the location of Gotham, Nottingham and York on a map.

Differentiated Individual/Paired/Group Work

- In groups, have pupils think about the ending of the folk tale. As a group, have them discuss what possible things might have happened to the cheeses.
- Ask pupils to pick their favourite event from the folk tale. They can illustrate this, give it a title and say why they like it the most.

Review

- Have each group feed back their predictions on where the cheeses had gone. Discuss the ideas of each group and ask pupils which ideas they think are the most likely/the least likely.

Comprehension

Introduction

- Pupils take it in turns to retell the folk tale 'The Cheeses That Ran Away' in their own words, sequencing the events correctly. The teacher should ask pupils to explain any vocabulary words that may be difficult for other pupils.

Development

- Discuss the comprehension activities on page 64, then allow pupils to complete the page independently.
- Compare their answers to questions 1, 3, 7 and 8, as these will have varied answers.
- Question 8 will provide an opportunity for pupils to use the ideas they discussed in groups in the first lesson.

Differentiated Individual/Paired/Group Work

- Pupils should work with a partner to write their own questions about the folk tale. Each set of pairs could swap their questions and answer the questions.
- Ask the pupils to think about other products the farmer from Gotham could sell at the market in future.

Review

- As a class, discuss the types of questions the pupils wrote in pairs. Were there any questions that the pupils could not answer from the text?

Word Reading

Teacher Information

- The activities on page 65 focus on common exception words, the 'ar' sound in 'farmer' and recognising singular and plural words.

Introduction

- Reread the text, but first explain to the pupils that the focus will be on words. While reading, ask pupils to circle the word 'farmer' every time it is mentioned.

Development

- Have pupils complete question 1 independently. Ensure that the pupils can read all the words. Discuss that these words are important words to be able to read and spell. Correct question 1 when all pupils have completed it.

- From the 'Introduction', pupils had to circle every time the word 'farmer' was present in the text (eight times). Have them look at the word 'farmer' and highlight and discuss the 'ar' sound. Have them read through the text quickly looking for any other words with the 'ar' sound ('market'). Have them complete questions 2, 3 and 4 independently. When correcting these questions ensure that pupils can sound out the words correctly.

- Revise singular and plural. Ensure pupils know what each word means. Ask them to scan quickly through the text and find one singular and one plural word. They should then attempt question 5 independently.

Differentiated Individual/Paired/Group Work

- In pairs, pupils can find ten singular words from the text. They must write the plural beside these words.

Review

- As a class, compare pupils' lists of ten singular words and their plurals. Revise the rules for singular and plural. Assign the words the pupils chose to the appropriate rule.

Assessment	
C3	Prepare a list of ten sentences that summarise the folk tale. Photocopy these sentences. Have pupils cut them out and sequence them in the correct order.
WR3	Ask pupils to spell the following 'ar' words. Call out each word slowly and emphasise the sounds: garden, shark, market, smart, park, start

Answers

Comprehension

1. Answers will vary but may include titles such as 'The Silly Cheese Man'.
2. A place where people get together to sell cheese, food and other things.
3. cows/milk
4. One of the cheeses rolled away by itself.
5. There was once
6. Answers will vary.
7. The cheeses were round and at the top of a hill.
8. Answers will vary.
9. places
10. hired

Word Reading

1. they/3, by/2, asked/3, where/1, his/6
2. Teacher check
3. (a) garden   (b) car   (c) smart
   (d) park   (e) shark   (f) mark
4. (a) park/start   (b) garden/park   (c) market
   (d) shark   (e) are   (f) car
5. (a) one   (b) more than one
   (c) more than one   (d) one

The Cheeses That Ran Away – 1

Read the folk tale.

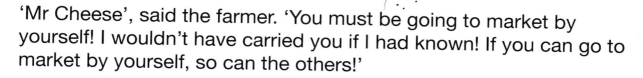

There was once a farmer from Gotham. He put his cheeses in a sack to take them to Nottingham market to sell.

The farmer carried the sack on his back. After a while, he got tired. He sat down at the top of a hill near Nottingham Bridge to rest.
When he got up to start on his way, one cheese fell out of the sack. It rolled down the hill towards the bridge.

'Mr Cheese', said the farmer. 'You must be going to market by yourself! I wouldn't have carried you if I had known! If you can go to market by yourself, so can the others!'

He took all the cheeses out of the sack. He rolled them down the hill. 'Meet me at the market place!' he shouted after them. Some cheeses rolled into a bush. Others rolled into another bush. The farmer did not see them. He walked happily to the market place to meet his cheeses.

The farmer looked for his cheeses all day. He asked others if they had seen them come to market.

'Who is bringing them?' asked the market man.

'They are bringing themselves. They know the way', the farmer said.

'Why aren't they here then?' asked the market man.

'Oh no!' said the farmer. 'They must have gone past the market place towards York!'

So the farmer hired a horse. He rode to York to find his cheeses. He did not find them. He never found out where the cheeses had gone.

My learning log	When I read this folk tale, I could read:	☐ all of it. ☐ most of it. ☐ parts of it.

The Cheeses That Ran Away – 2

1. Write another good title for the text.

   _____

2. What is a market?

   _____

3. Where does cheese come from? _____

4. What happened to make the farmer think the cheeses could take themselves to market?

   _____

   _____

5. What three words begin this folk tale?

   _____

6. Do you eat cheese? [Yes] [No] How do you like to eat it?

   _____

7. Why did the cheeses roll away?

   _____

8. What do you think happened to the cheeses?

   _____

   _____

9. Gotham, Nottingham and York are the names of ...

   _____.

10. Which word means 'paid money to use something for a short

    time'? _____

My learning log	While doing these activities:		
	I found Q _____ easy.	I found Q _____ tricky.	I found Q _____ fun.

The Cheeses That Ran Away – 3

1. How many times are these words found in the text?

they ☐   by ☐   asked ☐   where ☐   his ☐

2. Circle the words with the same sound as 'ar' as in 'farmer'.

| market | past | after | start | are | asked |

3. Write the 'ar' sound into these words. Read the words.

(a) g_____den   (b) c_____   (c) sm_____t

(d) p_____k   (e) sh_____k   (f) m_____k

4. Use the words from question 2 and question 3 to help you complete the sentences.

(a) Dad could not _____ the car.

(b) The flowers are growing in the _____.

(c) The farmer sold his vegetables at the _____.

(d) A _____ is a very dangerous creature.

(e) 'Where _____ you?' asked Mum.

(f) The _____ drove past the shop.

5. How many? Circle the box with the correct answer.

(a) bridge   one   more than one

(b) cheeses   one   more than one

(c) others   one   more than one

(d) man   one   more than one

| My learning log | Colour: | I can read 'smart', 'park' and 'garden'. | yes / no |
| | | I found question 5 easy. | yes / no |

The Rowan and the Pine

Teacher Information

Curriculum Links

Activity	Code	Objective	Outcome
Text	C7	• Draw on what they already know or on background information and vocabulary provided by the teacher	• Can discuss the changes in trees in the seasons
Comprehension	C10 C13	• Make inferences on the basis of what is being said and done • Explain clearly their understanding of what is read to them	• Can use what they have read to answer questions • Can discuss the main points of the narrative
Word Reading	WR1 WR2	• Apply phonic knowledge and skills as the route to decode words • Respond speedily with the correct sound to graphemes	• Can accurately identify syllables • Can read words with 'aw' like 'saw' • Can read words with 'ew' like 'flew'

Additional Teacher Information

Definition of Terms

Title
The name of a book, composition or other artistic work.

Narrative
A spoken or written account of connected events; a story. A narrative often consists of a framework with the following parts—a title, an orientation (setting, time, characters), a complication involving the main characters and a sequence of events, a resolution to a complication and an ending. A narrative may be written in the form of a poem, story, play, fairy tale, novel, myth, legend or ballad.

Links to other Curriculum Areas

• Science – Plants (Identify and name a variety of common wild and garden plants, including deciduous and evergreen trees; Identify and describe the basic structure of a variety of flowering plants, including trees); Seasonal changes (Observe changes across the four seasons)

Terminology for Pupils

narrative
word
title
capital letter
syllable

Suggested Reading

• *Red Leaf, Yellow Leaf* by Lois Ehlert
• *Winter Trees* by Carole Gerber (Some US trees included)
• *Crinkleroot's Guide to Knowing the Trees* by Jim Arnosky
• *Alfie's Long Winter* by Greg McEvoy
• *The Reasons for Seasons* by Gail Gibbons

Text

Teacher Information

- During the discussion of the text, encourage pupils to employ courteous listening skills such as turn-taking and listening to the points of views of others. This lesson also provides a great opportunity to link in a science lesson on the seasons and the effects on trees.

Introduction

- Have a discussion on the seasons. What season is it now? What months are in this season? What are the names of the other seasons? What type of weather do we expect in each season? How do the seasons affect nature, such as trees? Tell them that they are going to read a narrative about two trees in a forest and the effects of the seasons on them.

Development

- Read and discuss the text with the pupils. During discussion elicit the words 'deciduous' and 'evergreen' to distinguish between the two different types of trees. Assist the pupils with any unfamiliar words such as 'mountain', 'beautiful', 'branches' and 'skeleton'. This is a good opportunity to discuss singular and plural and to revise these concepts from previous lessons.

- Question pupils to gauge their understanding of what they have listened to or read. While reading, observe to see how pupils use phonic skills and knowledge to decode words. Assist pupils to decode more difficult words.

Differentiated Individual/Paired/Group Work

- Ask pupils to divide a sheet into four sections and write the seasons on top. Reading the narrative carefully, ask pupils to draw what the rowan and the pine tree looked like in each season.

- Highly confident readers could be asked to think about the story from the point of view of the rowan tree. What might the rowan be thinking about the pine tree during the four seasons? Have the pupils write one or two lines on the rowan tree's thoughts for each season.

Review

- Invite individual pupils to come up and show their drawings of the trees and their appearance in the different seasons. Ask the pupils to observe if any details have been left out.

Comprehension

Introduction

- Pupils take it in turns to retell the narrative 'The Rowan and the Pine'. The pupils must be encouraged to follow the sequence of the seasons (spring, summer, autumn and winter) in their retelling of the story. Ask pupils what they thought about the pine tree and his thoughts. Do they think he is selfish? kind? boastful? Ask the pupils to come up with a list of describing words.

Development

- Discuss the comprehension activities on page 70, then allow the pupils to complete the page independently.

- Compare their answers to question 7, which should generate a lot of discussion.

Differentiated Individual/Paired/Group Work

- Ask highly able readers to summarise the narrative in ten sentences; less able readers can summarise it in five sentences.

- In pairs, ask pupils to find out the names of some common trees. They can draw a picture of each one and draw a picture of its leaf. Ask them to find out if it is deciduous or evergreen.

Review

- Have pupils read out their summaries to the class. Other pupils can show their pictures of the trees they have researched.

Word Reading

Teacher Information

- The activities on page 71 focus on syllables, words with 'aw' such as in 'saw' and words with 'ew' such as in 'flew'.

Introduction

- Reread the text, but first explain to pupils that the focus will be on words. While reading, ask pupils to underline every time a season is mentioned.

Development

- Discuss and revise syllables. At this stage, pupils should be quite confident in using syllables. Pick out a number of words from the narrative and have pupils clap out the syllables of the words. On the board, divide these words with syllable lines to show pupils the syllables. For example, beau/ti/ful, proud/ly, for/est.

- Work with pupils on the 'aw' in words such as 'saw' and 'hawk'. Ensure pupils can hear the sound clearly.

- Question 6 requires pupils to examine words with 'ew' in them. Provide more words for extra practice (chew, drew, knew, nephew, stew, crew).

- Discuss the word reading activities on page 71, then allow pupils to complete the page independently.

Differentiated Individual/Paired/Group Work

- Use the text to revise singular and plural words. Ask pupils to make a list of words that add '-s' in the plural and words that add '-es' in the plural.

- Ask pupils to put the 'aw' words in questions 4 and 5 into sentences.

Review

- As a class, read some of the sentences pupils wrote for the 'aw' words.

- Ask a few pupils to spell the following 'aw' and 'ew' words: 'straw', 'grew', 'yawn', 'crawl' and 'knew'.

Assessment

C7	Ask pupils to write down the four seasons and one change that happens to a deciduous tree during each season.
WR1	Ask pupils to come up individually and read the following list of 'aw' and 'ew' words. Check to see if the pupil is applying phonic knowledge and skills to help them: awful, nephew, crew, dawn, prawn, grew, chew, fawn, lawn

Answers

Comprehension

1. (a) deciduous   (b) evergreen
2. a fruit with its seeds enclosed in a fleshy pulp
3. It had bare branches.
4. pine trees
5. It will grow new green leaves and white flowers.
6. Answers will vary.
7. Answers may include: The Two Trees, The Proud Pine and other suggestions from the pupils.
8. winter, spring, summer, autumn
9. The rowan grew bunches of bright red berries that made it look more beautiful.

Word Reading

1. spring, summer, autumn, winter
2. (a) beau/ti/ful – 3   (b) branch/es – 2
   (c) an/y/more – 3   (d) skel/e/ton – 3
3. (a) yes   (b) no   (c) no
   (d) yes   (e) yes   (f) yes
4. (a) draw   (b) crawl   (c) yawn
   (d) thaw   (e) hawk   (f) straw
5. raw, draw, drawing; lawn, dawn, yawn, yawned
6. grew, new; few, nephews, stew

The Rowan and the Pine – 1

Read the narrative.

In the forest on a mountain grew a tall pine tree. All year, the pine tree wore a beautiful coat of short, blue-green leaves. He thought he was the most beautiful tree in the forest.

In winter, the pine saw another tree growing nearby. The rowan tree had bare branches. In the falling snow, it looked like a skeleton.

'What a poor, sad tree!' thought the pine. 'It has no beautiful leaves to warm its branches.' He puffed up his own leaves proudly.

In spring, the pine tree looked at the rowan. It was covered in green leaves shaped like eagle feathers. There were white flowers too!

'What a nice tree!' thought the pine. 'He has no cones or seeds like me, but he looks better! But not as good as me!' He opened his cones and proudly spread black seeds far and wide.

In summer, the pine tree looked at the rowan. It had bunches of bright, red berries. He looked at his own green leaves.

'I'm not the most beautiful tree in the forest anymore!' he thought. 'All year, I am green ... green! Nothing changes!'

In autumn, the pine tree looked at the rowan. Its leaves were yellow and orange.

'What a beautiful tree! It is the most beautiful tree in the forest!' thought the pine sadly.

In winter, the pine looked at the rowan. Its yellow and orange leaves had fallen off. Its branches were bare again.

'What a poor, sad tree!' thought the pine. 'I am the most beautiful tree in the forest!' he said proudly.

My learning log	When I read this narrative, I could read:	☐ all of it. ☐ most of it. ☐ parts of it.

The Rowan and the Pine – 2

1. Circle the correct word.

    (a) A rowan is a | deciduous   evergreen | tree.

    (b) A pine is an | deciduous   evergreen | tree.

2. Berries are _____ .

3. Why did the rowan look like a skeleton?

_____

4. What will grow from pine cone seeds?

_____

5. What will happen to the rowan tree next spring?

_____

_____

6. Are there trees in your garden or at school? | Yes | | No |
What type of trees are they?

_____

7. Write another title for the narrative.

_____

8. Write the names of the four seasons of the year.

_____

9. What happened to make the pine think he was not the most beautiful tree in the forest?

_____

_____

My learning log	While doing these activities:		
	I found Q _____ easy.	I found Q _____ tricky.	I found Q _____ fun.

The Rowan and the Pine – 3

1. Write the names of the four seasons. (Remember the seasons don't have capital letters.)

   _____   _____

   _____   _____

2. How many syllables?

   (a) beautiful ☐   (b) branches ☐

   (c) anymore ☐   (d) skeleton ☐

3. Here are some words from the narrative. Are these words divided into the correct syllables? Tick or mark with an X.

   (a) for/est ☐   (b) a/no/ther ☐   (c) summe/r ☐

   (d) proud/ly ☐   (e) au/tumn ☐   (f) win/ter ☐

4. Write more words with 'aw' like 'saw'. Read each one.

   (a) dr_____   (b) cr_____l   (c) y_____n

   (d) th_____   (e) h_____k   (f) str_____

5. Follow the instructions and write the words.

Start with 'raw'.	
Add 'd' to the start.	
Add 'ing' to the end.	
The new word is:	

Start with 'lawn'.	
Change 'l' to 'd'.	
Change 'd' to 'y'.	
Add 'ed'.	
The new word is:	

6. Which words say 'ew' as in 'flew'? Draw a line under them.

   The rowan grew new green leaves in spring.

   My mum has a few nephews who love beef stew.

My learning log	Colour:	I know how many syllables are in *forest* and *another*.	yes / no
		I can read *straw*, *hawk* and *lawn*.	yes / no
		I can read *flew*, *nephew* and *stew*.	yes / no

Bonfire Night

Curriculum Links

Activity	Code	Objective	Outcome
Text	C2	• Be encouraged to link what they read or hear read to their own experiences	• Can discuss parts of a story with others
	C12	• Participate in discussion about what is read to them, taking turns and listening to what others say	• Can relate a theme to their own lives
Comprehension	C10	• Make inferences on the basis of what is being said and done	• Can infer from details in a text
	C13	• Explain clearly their understanding of what is read to them	• Can explain what they understand from a text
Word Reading	WR3	• Read accurately by blending sounds in unfamiliar words containing GPCs that have been taught	• Can read words with 'igh' like 'night'
	WR4	• Read common exception words, noting unusual correspondences between spelling and sound and where these occur in the word	• Can read common exception words such as 'children', 'people' and 'everyone'
	WR5	• Read words containing taught GPCs and -er and -est endings	• Can add -er and -est to words

Additional Teacher Information

Definition of Terms

Narrative
A spoken or written account of connected events; a story. A narrative often consists of a framework with the following parts—a title, an orientation (setting, time, characters), a complication involving the main characters and a sequence of events, a resolution to a complication and an ending. A narrative may be written in the form of a poem, story, play, fairy tale, novel, myth, legend or ballad.

Links to other Curriculum Areas

• History – Common words and phrases relating to the passing of time (today, soon, then); Changes within living memory revealing aspects of national life; significant events in their own locality

Terminology for Pupils

narrative
word
phrase
picture/illustration
noun
adjective
sentence

Suggested Reading

• *The Gunpowder Plot (How Do We Know About?)* by Deborah Fox (teacher background information)
• *Adventures in Sleepy Cove: Bonfire Night* by Joan Lee [Kindle Edition]
• *Hovis the Hedgehog: Bonfire Night* by Lynda Leigh-Crawford
• *Action Annie: Story Twelve – Annie's Bonfire* by William Forde [Kindle Edition]
• *Secret Seven 11: Seven Secret Fireworks* by Enid Blyton (a chapter book to read to the pupils over time)

72 · · · · · · · · *Reading – Comprehension and Word Reading* · · · · · · · · · · · · · · · · ·Prim-Ed Publishing · · · · www.prim-ed.com

Text

Teacher Information

- Guy Fawkes Night, Bonfire Night or Fireworks Night is celebrated on 5 November. It commemorates the arrest of Guy Fawkes, who was involved in the Gunpowder Plot to blow up the House of Lords in 1605, in an attempt to assassinate King James I and the members of parliament. An effigy, or guy, made from old clothes stuffed with paper or straw is burned on the bonfire. Parkin Cake (a soft cake made from oatmeal, ginger, treacle and syrup), baked potatoes, soup, sausages and toasted marshmallows are eaten.

Introduction

- Discuss with the pupils if they have seen a bonfire. Ask them when they usually see one. Discuss issues of safety and protection. Ask them if they have heard of Bonfire Night. Do they know when it is? Ask some pupils to relate their experiences to the class. Explain that today they are going to read a narrative about two children who go out to celebrate Bonfire Night.

Development

- Read and discuss the text with the pupils. Assist them with any unfamiliar words such as 'neighbourhood', 'asked', 'whining', 'scarecrow', 'noise', 'marshmallows' and 'watched'. Question pupils to gauge their understanding of what they have listened to or read. While reading, observe to see how pupils use phonic skills and knowledge to decode words.
- Assist pupils to decode more difficult words.
- If reading the text together as a class, correct inaccurate reading.
- During reading or listening to the narrative, emphasise the direct speech by using a different tone of voice for the narrative passages. In this way, the pupils will hear how fluent, confident readers read.

Differentiated Individual/Paired/Group Work

- Ask pupils to list the things mentioned in the narrative that are done on Bonfire Night.
- In pairs, pupils describe for each other their memories of Bonfire Night. What did they do? Did they do anything different to Toby and Ella?
- Highly confident readers could write their memories of a Bonfire Night celebration.

Review

- Ask pupils to have a class discussion based on the story. Remind them to employ courteous listening skills, such as turn-taking and listening to the points of views of others.

Comprehension

Introduction

- Pupils take it in turns to recall the events of the narrative 'Bonfire Night' in their own words, sequencing the events correctly.

Development

- Discuss the comprehension activities on page 76, then allow the pupils to complete the page independently.
- Compare their answers to question 4, as this will have varied answers. This question requires the pupil to infer from details implied in the text. Ask the pupils to give reasons to support their answers.

Differentiated Individual/Paired/Group Work

- Have pupils work in groups. Ask them to think of other events throughout the year (Halloween, Christmas, St Patrick's Day). Assign a celebration/event/festival to each group and ask them to work together to think of all the traditional activities done on these days.

Review

- As a whole class, discuss the work each group has done on the different celebration/event/festival. Discuss each of these in detail. If time allows, create a display chart on each celebration/event/festival.

Word Reading

Teacher Information

- The activities on page 77 focus on common exception words, -er, -est and –tch endings and words with 'igh' such as 'night'.

Introduction

- Reread the text, but this time let pupils know that the focus will be on words. While reading, ask pupils to underline any words that are the names of clothes.

Development

- Questions 1 and 2 ask pupils to find words that end in '-ss' and also some common exception words such as 'children', 'people' and 'everyone'. Make sure pupils can read these words and discuss the spelling of these words.

- Questions 3 to 6 focus on adding word elements. Ensure pupils can read the word endings carefully before they add them.

- Questions 7 and 8 focus on words with 'igh' like 'night'. Discuss this sound, often called the long 'i' sound. Pupils may have encountered the other way long 'i' can be written (i-e). If they have, compare the two ways of representing this sound.

- Discuss the word reading activities on page 77, then allow the pupils to complete the page independently.

Differentiated Individual/Paired/Group Work

- In pairs, pupils can reread the text underlining 'igh' words that are contained within it.

- Less able readers would benefit from intensive practice on the long 'i' sound, spelt 'igh'. The teacher should provide many other words for practice (sigh, sight, might, midnight, daylight, fright).

- Highly able readers can write the words in question 7 in sentences. Challenge them to use two or three 'igh' words in the same sentence.

Review

- As a whole class, discuss any question on page 77 that caused problems or difficulties. Are there any questions that the class feel they need more practice on?

Assessment

C2	Ask pupils to write a short paragraph called 'My Memories of Bonfire Night'. When examining the passage, check that pupils are including details from their own lives. Check to see if they are applying learned phonic knowledge and using common exception words correctly. Note common areas of difficulty for future lessons.
WR3	Ask pupils to put the following words into sentences to show their meaning: might, bright, light, flight, midnight

Answers

Comprehension

1. The pupils may be familiar with the names Guy Fawkes Night or Fireworks Night.
2. Answers may include:
   5 November, November, autumn
3. grumbling
4. Yes, because he liked it.
5. the bonfire
6. baked potatoes, hot dogs, toasted marshmallows
7. Teacher check

Word Reading

1. dress, hiss
2. children (1), people (2), everyone (2)
3. jumper
4. (a) colder   (b) darker
5. (a) coldest   (b) darkest
6. (a) catch   (b) hutch   (c) notch
   (d) witch   (e) fetch   (f) watch
7. (a) high   (b) light   (c) might
   (d) bright   (e) right   (f) flight
8. (a) light, bright   (b) high   (c) right, might

Bonfire Night – 1

Read the narrative.

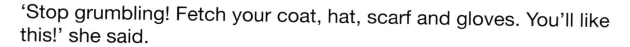

'Where are we going, Ella?' asked Toby. 'It's cold outside. It's getting dark.'

'Today's 5 November', said Ella, as if that answered Toby's question. 'It's better when it's cold and dark!'

'I want to stay inside near the fire', wailed Toby.

'Stop grumbling! Fetch your coat, hat, scarf and gloves. You'll like this!' she said.

Toby got his warm clothes and Ella helped him dress.

'Where are we going?' asked Toby again. 'It's cold. I want to stay inside!'

'Stop whining!' Ella said. 'Let's go!' She pulled Toby after her and followed her mum and dad outside and down the street.

The children and their parents hurried to the park. Many people in the town had gathered around a large bonfire. The flames jumped high into the air. Toby saw two men throw a funny-looking scarecrow onto the bonfire. Sparks flew and the 'guy' burned. Everyone cheered.

Soon a rainbow of fireworks leapt across the sky. Showers of colour filled the sky. 'Pop! Bang! Hiss!' The fireworks made lots of noise. No-one spoke. Everyone watched the display. Then the fireworks died away. People hurried around the bonfire.

'Here, Toby!' said Ella. 'Try a baked potato or a hot dog! There are toasted marshmallows too! You'll like this!'

And he did! He liked *everything* about Bonfire Night!

My learning log	When I read this narrative, I could read:	☐ all of it. ☐ most of it. ☐ parts of it.

Bonfire Night – 2

1. What is another name for Bonfire Night?

   _____

2. What time of year is Bonfire Night held? _____

3. Which word in the text that starts with 'gr' means 'complaining

   in a rumbling sound'? _____

4. Do you think Toby will want to go to the next Bonfire Night?

   (Yes) (No) Why? _____

   _____

5. What thing do these words and phrases tell about?

flames jumped high into the air	sparks flew
'guy' burned _____	

6. What food is eaten on Bonfire Night?

   _____

7. Draw and label a picture about Bonfire Night.

   [   ]

My learning log	While doing these activities:		
	I found Q _____ easy.	I found Q _____ tricky.	I found Q _____ fun.

Bonfire Night – 3

1. Write two words ending with '-ss'.

   _____   _____

2. How many times can you find these words in the narrative?

   children ☐   people ☐   everyone ☐

3. Change '-ed' in 'jumped' to '-er' to make a noun.

   _____

4. Add '-er' to make new adjectives.
   Read the new words.

   (a) cold _____   (b) dark _____

5. Add '-est' to make new adjectives. Read the new words.

   (a) cold _____   (b) dark _____

6. Add '-tch' to make more words like 'fetch'. Read them.

   (a) ca_____   (b) hu_____   (c) no_____

   (d) wi_____   (e) fe_____   (f) wa_____

7. Write more words with 'igh' like 'night'. Read each one.

   (a) h_____   (b) l_____t   (c) m_____t

   (d) br_____t   (e) r_____t   (f) fl_____t

8. Fill in these sentences using words from question 7.

   (a) The new _____ bulb was very _____.

   (b) That mountain is very _____.

   (c) If I get all my sums _____,

       I _____ get a nice treat!

My learning log	Colour:	I can read the words *children*, *people* and *everyone*.	yes / no
		I can read all the words in question 6.	yes / no
		I can read all the words in question 7.	yes / no

The Four Seasons

Read the report.

In most places the year is split up into four seasons—spring, summer, autumn and winter. The seasons last for three months. They are caused because of the way the earth moves around the sun.

Spring

March, April and May are the spring months. The weather is getting warmer. Deciduous trees grow new leaves. Flowers bloom. Bees and butterflies buzz around them. Many baby animals are born. Spring bulbs like daffodils pop up. There may be rain showers.

Summer

Summer is the hottest time of the year. June, July and August are the summer months. In summer people like to go swimming at the beach. It is a hot, sunny season. The days are long. There may be thunderstorms.

Autumn

September, October and November are the autumn months. It is cooler. The days may be cold and dry or rainy and windy. People wear warmer clothes. Deciduous trees lose their leaves. The days are getting shorter.

Winter

Winter is a very cold and wet time of the year. December, January and February are the winter months. There may be ice, rain, snow, sleet and wind. People wear warm clothes. Some animals hibernate (sleep) until the warmer months come. The days are short.

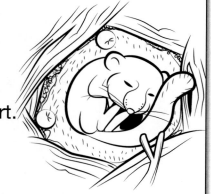

The Four Seasons

1. Which season is usually hot and sunny?

   ☐ spring

   ☐ summer

   ☐ autumn

   ☐ winter

   1 mark

2. Match the season to its description.

   (a) getting cooler   •   •   spring

   (b) getting warmer   •   •   autumn

   1 mark

3. A season is _____

   _____.

   2 marks

4. In which season would you wear the lightest clothes?

   ☐ spring

   ☐ summer

   ☐ autumn

   ☐ winter

   1 mark

5. Which season comes next?

   spring, summer, autumn, _____

   1 mark

   Total for this page   /6

The Four Seasons

1. Write the root word for each adjective.

   (a) warmer   _____

   (b) swimming   _____

   (c) shorter   _____

   1 mark

2. Which word has three syllables?

   showers   ☐

   hibernate ☐

   sleet   ☐

   deciduous ☐

   1 mark

3. Find and copy two compound words from the text.

   (a) It is made up of the words 'storms' and 'thunder'.

   _____

   (b) It is made up of the words 'flies' and 'butter'.

   _____

   1 mark

4. Write the plural of each word.

   (a) beach   _____

   (b) sun   _____

   (c) animal   _____

   1 mark

Total for this page	/4	Total for this assessment	/10

The Four Seasons

Genre: Report

Breakdown of question type/content and mark allocation

Comprehension		Word Reading	
Q 1. Finding information	1 mark	**Q 1.** Root words	1 mark
Q 2. Matching	1 mark	**Q 2.** Syllables	1 mark
Q 3. Identifying the main idea	2 marks	**Q 3.** Compound words	1 mark
Q 4. Inferring	1 mark	**Q 4.** Plurals	1 mark
Q 5. Sequencing	1 mark		
Sub-total		Sub-total	
		Record the pupil's total result for this assessment.	

Assessment Answers

Assessment – The Four Seasons

Comprehension .... *Page 79*

1. summer
2. (a) getting cooler—autumn
   (b) getting warmer—spring
3. A season is a time of the year that covers three months and has special weather conditions.
4. summer
5. winter

Word Reading .... *Page 80*

1. (a) warm   (b) swim   (c) short
2. hibernate
3. (a) thunderstorms   (b) butterflies
4. (a) beaches   (b) suns   (c) animals

Creatures of the Oceans

Teacher Information

Curriculum Links

Activity	Code	Objective	Outcome
Text	C1	• Listen to and discuss a wide range of non-fiction at a level beyond that at which they can read independently	• Can extract information from a report
	C6	• Discuss word meanings, linking new meanings to those already known	• Can understand and discuss the meanings of words
	C7	• Draw on what they already know or on background information and vocabulary provided by the teacher	
Comprehension	C8	• Check that the text makes sense to them as they read and correct inaccurate reading	• Can check if their reading makes sense
	C13	• Explain clearly their understanding of what is read to them	• Can pick out the main points of information from a report
Word Reading	WR1 WR3	• Apply phonic knowledge and skills as the route to decode words • Read accurately by blending sounds in unfamiliar words containing GPCs that have been taught	• Can read words with a variety of consonant blends • Can use the prefix 'un-'

Additional Teacher Information

Definition of Terms

Text
A book or other written or printed work, regarded in terms of its content rather than its physical form.

Story
An account of imaginary or real people and events told for entertainment.

Report
A report is a written document describing the findings of an individual or group. A report may take the form of a newspaper report, sports or police report, or a report about an animal, person or object.

Links to other Curriculum Areas

• Geography – Locational knowledge (name and locate the world's five oceans); Human and physical geography (use basic geographical vocabulary to refer to sea and ocean)

• Science – Animals, including humans (Identify and name a variety of common animals including fish, reptiles and mammals; Identify and name a variety of common animals that are carnivores, herbivores and omnivores)

Terminology for Pupils

report
text
information
story
word
prefix
consonant
syllable

Suggested Reading

• *National Geographic Little Kids First Big Book of the Ocean (First Big Books)* by Catherine D. Hughes
• *Eye Wonder: Ocean* by Prentice Hall
• *Over in the Ocean: In a Coral Reef* by Marianne Berkes
• *Commotion in the Ocean* by Giles Andreae

82 • • • • • • • • • *Reading – Comprehension and Word Reading* • Prim-Ed Publishing • • • • www.prim-ed.com

Text

Teacher Information

- There are a lot of names of sea creatures in this report. Having access to an Internet search engine or children's encyclopaedias would be useful.

Introduction

- Have a discussion about the oceans and seas and elicit from the pupils any sea creatures that they know of. Have a discussion on these. Typical animals mentioned may be the whale or the dolphin. Have pictures of the catfish, walrus, green turtle, sea otter and blue whale. Tell pupils that they will read a report and they will discover a lot of new information about these sea creatures.

Development

- Read and discuss the text with the pupils. Assist them with any unfamiliar words such as 'bony', 'mussels', 'algae', 'mammals', 'abalone', 'urchins', 'shellfish' and 'krill'. Question pupils to gauge their understanding of what they have listened to or read. While reading, observe to see how pupils use phonic skills and knowledge to decode words. Assist pupils to decode more difficult words.

- Discuss the similarities and differences among the five animals and whether they are carnivores, herbivores or omnivores.

- If reading the text together as a class, correct inaccurate reading.

- A class world map, if available, may be referred to when the five oceans are mentioned.

Differentiated Individual/Paired/Group Work

- Assign different groups a sea creature from the report and ask each group to find out some extra information on the creature. Have them draw a picture of each creature and list some of the information they have found. Children's fact books and encyclopaedias would be useful resources here.

- Individual pupils could be asked to place the following words in their own sentences: whiskers, fins, flippers, mammals.

- In pairs, pupils can discuss other mammals they are familiar with. They may have read Unit 9 'Hedgehogs' already and they can try and compare creatures of the oceans with land mammals. This might tie in with a science lesson.

Review

- Each group can discuss and present the extra information they have learned about their sea creature to the rest of the class.

Comprehension

Teacher Information

- Question 1 requires that pupils use the text to find the location of the various sea creatures. Even though the text provides the information, it might be worthwhile to look at the different ocean areas on a map or globe.

Introduction

- The teacher should revise the main points of the lesson, talking about each sea creature in turn (catfish, walrus, green turtle, sea otter and blue whale). The teacher should establish what the pupils can recall and explain about each creature.

Development

- Discuss the comprehension activities on page 86, then allow the pupils to complete the page independently.

- Compare their answers to questions 6, 7 and 8 as these may have varied answers.

Differentiated Individual/Paired/Group Work

- Pupils could be asked to write a short summary on each sea creature.

- Less able readers could be asked to write one full sentence on each creature; highly capable readers could write four or five sentences on each.

Review

- As a class, compare pupils' summaries and see if they have succeeded in including all the main points.

Word Reading

Teacher Information

- The activities on page 87 focus on the prefix 'un-', consonant blends and syllables.

Introduction

- Reread the text with the pupils, but first explain that the focus will be on words. While reading the text, ask pupils to underline any words starting with 'cr' (creatures, crabs).

Development

- Teach pupils the word 'prefix'. Explain to them that prefixes are added on to the start of a word and they can change the meaning. Explain that one of the most common prefixes is 'un-' and that it can make the word meaning opposite. Illustrate with several oral examples first and use words that the pupils are familiar with. Then write the words on the board without the prefix. Show pupils that adding 'un-' creates the opposite. For example, happy – unhappy, fair – unfair. Ask pupils to look at paragraph 1 and to locate the word that has the prefix 'un-' (unlike).

- Have pupils complete questions 1 to 4 independently. Correct these.

- Before allowing pupils to complete question 5, ensure that pupils can sound out each blend. Can they orally think of any words that begin with these blends? Have pupils complete question 5 independently and correct it.

- Question 6 focuses on syllables. Revise the work covered on syllables from previous units. Have pupils complete question 6 independently.

Differentiated Individual/Paired/Group Work

- Ask pupils to place the words in question 3 into sentences. Challenge highly confident readers to use both the root word and the prefixed word in the same sentence (e.g. I was lucky in the raffle, but my brother was unlucky and didn't win a prize.)

- Highly confident readers could try to add five or more words to each box in question 5. These words can be any words the pupils know or have met in the past. Less confident readers can add a few words to each box (teacher assistance may be needed with spelling).

Review

- As a class, ask pupils to take it in turns to call out some of the words they have added to each box. The teacher can act as a scribe and create a list on the board or on charts of each consonant blend.

Assessment

C13	Ask each pupil to pick any sea creature from the report. Ask them to write some information that they have learned about this creature. Ask them to draw an illustration.
WR1	Provide the pupils with the following list of words (only some of which can take the prefix 'un-'). Ask the pupils to add the prefix 'un-' to the correct words: danger, use, kind, fish, like, live, safe, swim, lucky, fair. They could then place each prefixed word in a sentence.

Answers

Comprehension

1. Teacher check
2. catfish, walrus, sea otter
3. sea otter
4. gives information
5. (a) gills (b) whalebone
6. They will die out.
7. No—Catfish and sea otters eat snails, so they must live in the ocean, too.
8. Answers may include; cow, buffalo, camel, elephant, elk, hippopotamus, reindeer, rhinoceros

Word Reading

1. un-
2. not like
3. (a) unkind (b) unlucky (c) unsafe
   (d) unfair (e) unfriendly (f) unlike
4. (a) unlucky (b) unfair (c) unsafe
5. sc–scales, gr–grasses/green, cr–crabs/creatures, cl–clams, kr–krill, sn–snails, fl–flippers, sm–small, sw–swim
6. (a) At/lan/tic (b) In/di/an

Creatures of the Oceans – 1

Read the report.

Many interesting animals live in the seas and oceans around the world.

Catfish live in the **Atlantic Ocean**. They have whiskers. They have a bony head for digging up insects, snails and worms from the bottom of the ocean. They have fins to help them swim and gills to breathe like other fish. Unlike other fish, they have no scales. They are eaten for food.

The walrus lives in the **Arctic Ocean**. It is a mammal. It has flippers, a large head, small eyes, tusks and whiskers. A walrus uses its whiskers to find clams, mussels and other animals on the bottom of the ocean to eat. It eats fish, too.

The green turtle lives in the **Indian Ocean**. It has a hard shell where it can hide. It has flippers, a tail and lays eggs. It eats crabs, jellyfish, baby sea animals, sea grasses and algae. Green turtles are in danger of dying out.

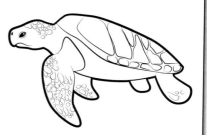

Sea otters live in the **Pacific Ocean**. They are mammals. They have lots of fur and whiskers. They eat urchins, abalone, mussels, clams, crabs and snails. They are good divers. They use small rocks to open shellfish.

The blue whale lives in the **Southern Ocean**. These mammals are the largest and loudest animals in the world. They eat tiny sea animals called krill. They catch them in hair-like teeth called whalebone. They have babies called calves. They can live for over a hundred years.

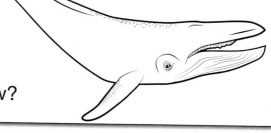

What interesting sea creatures do you know?

My learning log	When I read this report, I could read:	☐ all of it.	☐ most of it.	☐ parts of it.

Creatures of the Oceans – 2

1. Draw a line to show where each animal lives on the map.

   catfish   •

   walrus   •

   green turtle   •

   sea otter   •

   blue whale   •

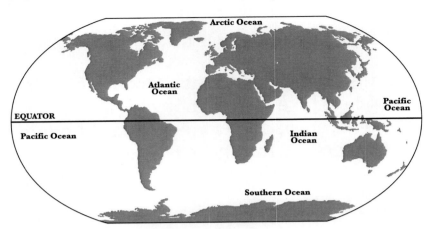

2. Which three animals in the text have whiskers?

   _____   _____   _____

3. Which animal uses a tool to get food?

   _____

4. This text …   gives information ⬜.   tells a story ⬜.

5. Which word means:

   (a) the body part fish use to breathe?   _____

   (b) hair-like teeth of a blue whale?   _____

6. What will happen if we don't look after green turtles?

   _____

7. Do snails only live on the land in gardens? [Yes] [No]
   How do you know?

   _____

8. Which land animals have babies called calves?

   _____

My learning log	While doing these activities:		
	I found Q _____ easy.	I found Q _____ tricky.	I found Q _____ fun.

Creatures of the Oceans – 3

1. Write the prefix at the beginning of 'unlike'. _____

2. The prefix 'un-' in 'unhappy' makes the word mean 'not happy'.

   What does the word 'unlike' mean?   not _____

3. Add 'un-' to these words.

   (a) kind   _____   (b) lucky _____

   (c) safe   _____   (d) fair   _____

   (e) friendly _____   (f) like   _____

4. Circle the correct word.

   (a) He never wins anything. He is very   [unlike]   [unlucky].

   (b) The referee in the football match was very   [unfair]   [unlike].

   (c) The busy road was   [unkind]   [unsafe].

5. Write one word from the text beginning with each pair of consonants.

sc	gr	cr
cl	kr	sn
fl	sm	sw

6. Write each word correctly in the syllable box.

   (a) Atlantic

   (b) Indian

My learning log	*Colour:*	I know how to use the prefix 'un-'.	yes / no
		I can think of words that start with 'gr' and 'sc'.	yes / no

Prim-Ed Publishing • • • www.prim-ed.com • *Reading – Comprehension and Word Reading* • • • • • • • • **87**

Curriculum Links

Activity	Code	Objective	Outcome
Text	C1 C5	• Listen to and discuss a wide range of poems at a level beyond that at which they can read independently • Learn to appreciate rhymes and poems	• Can read a factual poem • Can recognise rhyming words
Comprehension	C6 C13	• Discuss word meanings, linking new meanings to those already known • Explain clearly their understanding of what is read to them	• Can discuss vocabulary from the poem • Can answer questions about the poem
Word Reading	WR2 WR5	• Respond speedily with the correct sound to graphemes • Read words containing taught GPCs and -er and -est endings	• Can read words with 'ur' such as 'turn' • Can add '-er' and '-est' to adjectives

Additional Teacher Information

Definition of Terms

Text
A book or other written or printed work, regarded in terms of its content rather than its physical form.

Poem
A piece of writing in which the expression of feelings and ideas is given intensity by particular attention to diction (sometimes involving rhyme), rhythm and imagery.

Diagram
A simplified drawing showing the appearance, structure or workings of something; a schematic representation.

Links to other Curriculum Areas

• Science – Seasonal changes (Observe changes across the four seasons; Observe and describe weather associated with the seasons and how day length varies)

Terminology for Pupils

poem
diagram
word
sentence
text
title
rhyme
compound word
adjective

Suggested Reading

• *Day and Night* and *Seasons of the Year (Patterns in Nature series)* by Margaret Hall
• *What Makes Day and Night?* and *Sunshine Makes the Seasons (Let's-Read-and-Find-Out Science 2)* by Franklyn M. Branley
• *I am Afraid of the Dark (Good Night books, Ages 2–6. The Adventures of Robin and Sunbeam series, ebook 1)* [Kindle Edition] by Mira Drori

Text

Teacher Information

- This poem gives information about sunbeams. It provides a great stimulus for a lesson in either science or geography.

Introduction

- Discuss the importance of the sun. Elicit from pupils the role they think the sun plays for us on Earth. Read *Day and Night* and *Seasons of the Year* by Margaret Hall to stimulate thought and discussion.

Development

- Read and discuss the poem with the pupils. Assist them with any unfamiliar words such as 'bright', 'earth', 'shining' and 'done'.
- Question pupils to gauge their understanding of what they have listened to or read. It may be necessary to use a torch and a ball to demonstrate night and day and the seasons to ensure complete understanding.
- While reading, observe to see how pupils use phonic skills and knowledge to decode words. Assist pupils to decode more difficult words.
- Emphasise rhyming words during reading. If reading the text together as a class, correct inaccurate reading.
- It is important for pupils to realise that diagrams as well as print can convey information.

Differentiated Individual/Paired/Group Work

- In pairs, have pupils ask each other to find a matching rhyming word in the poem. For example, partner A asks partner B to find a rhyming words for 'faces' ('places'). They then work together to try to come up with more words that rhyme with those two words. Then partner B picks another word from the poem and they continue with this system.
- Challenge highly confident readers to find five words with one syllable and five words with more than one syllable. They should make a list showing these words.
- Less able readers will need help with the poem so the teacher could work with a small group, working on each stanza in detail, providing reading practice and support.

Review

- As a class, discuss the rhyming words that the pairs thought of. Discuss the spelling patterns that can be seen.

Comprehension

Teacher Information

- Questions 7 and 8 will involve a lot of personal responses from the pupils.

Introduction

- Pupils discuss what they remember reading in the poem. Can they recall how day becomes night? What happens in summer? What happens in winter? Ask pupils to recall some of the rhyming words.

Development

- Discuss the comprehension activities on page 92, then allow the pupils to complete the page independently.
- Compare and discuss their answers to questions 7 and 8.

Differentiated Individual/Paired/Group Work

- In pairs, have pupils write the answers to the following questions in the form of a report. Ask them to use the poem to provide them with the information.
  - How does day become night?
  - What happens in summer?
  - What happens in winter?
- In groups, ask pupils to think about their favourite seasons. Each group must come up with five reasons why the season they have chosen is the best season. They should illustrate their responses.

Review

- As a class, listen to pupils read out their reports on the three questions. Discuss any questions they found difficult to answer.

Word Reading

Teacher Information

- The activities on page 93 focus on rhyming words, compound words, adding '-er' and '-est' to words and words with 'ur' as in 'turn'.

Introduction

- Reread the text, but first explain to the pupils that the focus will be on words. While reading, ask the pupils to underline every time the word 'earth' is mentioned (seven times).

Development

- Discuss again the rhyming words that are found in the poem. Ensure that pupils can see the part of each word that provides the rhyming part.
- Revise compound words. This has been covered in other units. Ask pupils to suggest some common compound words.
- Pupils have also had considerable practice adding '-er' and '-est' to words. Revise what they remember about adding these endings.
- Discuss the 'ur' in 'turns'. Emphasise the sound these two letters make. Can the pupils think of other words that have this sound? Make a list on the board.
- Discuss the word reading activities on page 93, then allow pupils to complete the page independently.

Differentiated Individual/Paired/Group Work

- In pairs, pupils can be asked to create a poem of their own using some of the rhyming words they have met in this unit. The poems can be very short in length.
- Ask pupils to place the words in question 6 into sentences.
- Ask pupils to find out and write down a list of all the planets in our solar system.

Review

- As a class, invite some of the pairs to read out the poems that they have written. Have a class vote to see which poem the class thinks is the best.

Assessment	
C5	Ask each pupil to say and write a rhyming word for the following words. (Do not say them aloud for the pupil; allow the pupil to read them and then respond): night, long, sun, faces, star Note as part of the assessment how well each pupil spelt these rhyming words.
WR2	Have pupils read the following words: purple, church, Thursday, hurt, nurse, turkey, burst

Answers

Comprehension

1. Teacher check
2. (a) away from   (b) towards
3. a star
4. Answers will vary.
5. The earth spins around the sun.
6. (a) star   (b) run/fun/done
7. Answers may include:
   The earth would not have days, nights and seasons;
   Some places would always be hot;
   Some places would always be cold;
   Some places would always have days;
   Some places would always have night.
8. Answers will vary.

Word Reading

1. light, flight, bright, night; star, far; long, strong; sun, run, fun, done; faces, places
2. (a) sunshine   (b) sunlight
3. -er
4. (a) lighter   (b) stronger   (c) shorter   (d) warmer
5. (a) longest   (b) brightest
6. (a) hurt   (b) church   (c) burst
   (d) Thursday   (e) nurse   (f) purple
7. (a) nurse   (b) Thursday   (c) purple   (d) church

Sunbeams – 1

Read the poem.

Every day before it's light

Sunbeams begin their very long flight.

They leave the sun and travel far

To warm the earth from the sun—our star.

In winter, the earth spins away from the sun.

The sunbeams have a longer way to run.

The sunbeams are not very strong.

The days are short. The
nights are long.

In summer, the earth spins
towards the sun.

The sunbeams can have lots of fun.

The way is short. The sunbeams are bright.

The earth gets hot with long days of light.

Every day changes into night.

The earth turns away from the sun's bright light.

The sunbeams hide their shining faces

Until a new day lights up earth's places.

The earth keeps spinning around the sun

Days after nights until the seasons are done.

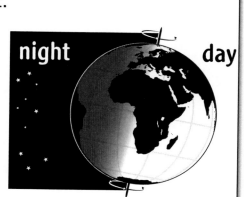

My learning log	When I read this poem, I could read:	☐ all of it. ☐ most of it. ☐ parts of it.

Prim-Ed Publishing • • • www.prim-ed.com • *Reading – Comprehension and Word Reading* • • • • • • • • 91

Sunbeams – 2

1. Write 'day' and 'night' on the diagram.

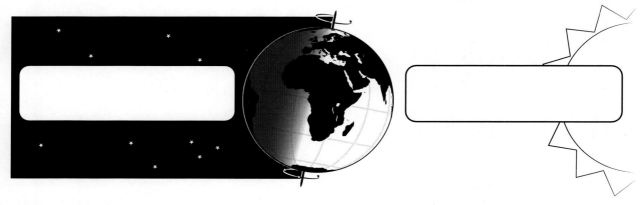

2. Write words to finish the sentences.

    (a) In winter, the earth is facing _____ the sun.

    (b) In summer, the earth is facing _____ the sun.

3. What space object is the sun? _____

4. Write a new title for the text.

    _____

5. What does the earth do to make days, nights and seasons?

    _____

6. Write words from the poem that rhyme with each word.

    (a) far _____   (b) sun _____

7. What would happen if the earth stopped spinning around the sun?

    _____

8. Which season do you like best? _____

    Why? _____

    _____

My learning log	While doing these activities:		
	I found Q _____ easy.	I found Q _____ tricky.	I found Q _____ fun.

Sunbeams – 3

1. Find the rhyming words in the poem for the following words.

light	star	long	sun	faces
_____	_____	_____	_____	_____
_____			_____	
_____				

2. Write compound words like 'sunbeam' (sun + beam).

   (a) sun + shine _____

   (b) sun + light _____

3. What has been added to 'long' to make

   the adjective 'longer'? _____

4. Add '-er' to make adjectives.

   (a) light _____   (b) strong _____

   (c) short _____   (d) warm _____

5. Add '-est' to make adjectives.

   (a) long _____   (b) bright _____

6. Write 'ur' like in 'turns' into these words. Read them.

   (a) h_____t   (b) ch_____ch   (c) b_____st

   (d) Th_____sday   (e) n_____se   (f) p_____ple

7. Read the clues and write the 'ur' word.

   (a) Someone who works in a hospital. _____

   (b) A day of the week, but not Saturday. _____

   (c) A colour. _____

   (d) A place where people pray and sing. _____

My learning log	*Colour:*	I know what a compound word is.	yes / no
		I can read words like *church, purple* and *nurse*.	yes / no

How to Make Porridge

Curriculum Links

Activity	Code	Objective	Outcome
Text	C2 C6	• Be encouraged to link what they read or hear read to their own experiences • Discuss word meanings, linking new meanings to those already known	• Can read a recipe • Can explain common words found in a recipe
Comprehension	C8 C13	• Check that the text makes sense to them as they read and correct inaccurate reading • Explain clearly their understanding of what is read to them	• Can understand a set of instructions • Can retell a recipe in their own words
Word Reading	WR1 WR2 WR3	• Apply phonic knowledge and skills as the route to decode words • Respond speedily with the correct sound to graphemes • Read accurately by blending sounds in unfamiliar words containing GPCs that have been taught	• Can read words with 'nk' in them • Can read words with 'oa' like 'oats' • Can read words with 'ew' like 'flew'

Additional Teacher Information

Definition of Terms

Title
The name of a book, composition or other artistic work.

Recipe
A recipe is a procedure or set of instructions for preparing a particular dish, including a list of the ingredients required. A procedure tells how to make or do something. It uses clear, concise language and command verbs. A recipe is an informational text.

Links to other Curriculum Areas

• Personal, social, health and economic education (PSHE) – Diet for a healthy lifestyle
• Mathematics – Measurement (measuring mass/weight and capacity in grams and millilitres)

Terminology for Pupils

recipe
title
sound
syllable
word
rhyming word

Suggested Reading

• *The Magic Porridge Pot* by Paul Galdone
• *The Tomtes' Christmas Porridge* by Sven Nordqvist
• *Pirates Eat Porridge* by Christopher Morgan (a story to listen to)

Text

Teacher Information

- Pinhead or steel-cut oatmeal is the whole grain oat cut into pieces. It is not the same as rolled oats. Steel-cut oatmeal takes longer to cook than rolled or instant oats, has a nuttier flavour and is chewier.

- The spurtle (or spirtle) is a very old Scottish kitchen tool used for flipping oatcakes. It was originally a flat, wooden tool like a spatula. Over time, it was used solely for stirring oatmeal and soup, and became more rod-shaped like a fat piece of dowel with a contoured end for gripping.

- There are some interesting traditions associated with porridge making. Porridge was always stirred clockwise with the right hand (to avoid the Devil coming for the stirrer); it was served in wooden bowls and eaten standing up; a bowl of cream sat in the middle of the table for each person to dip their spoonful of porridge into before eating; it was stirred with a spurtle; left-over porridge was allowed to get cold after being poured into containers, cut up into portions, wrapped and taken to work for eating as lunch, dinner or a snack the following day.

Introduction

- Ask pupils about what they eat for breakfast. Ask them if they have ever eaten porridge. Explain that today they will read a recipe for porridge.

Development

- Read and discuss the text with the pupils. Assist them with any unfamiliar words such as units of measure, or the list of ingredients.

- Question pupils to gauge their understanding of what they have listened to or read.

- While reading, observe and listen to see how pupils use phonic skills and knowledge to decode words. Assist pupils with more difficult words.

- If reading the recipe together as a class, correct inaccurate reading.

Differentiated Individual/Paired/Group Work

- Ask pupils to work in pairs to list the ingredients and then to illustrate each step of the recipe.

- Allow highly able readers to research their favourite breakfast recipe and to make a list of the ingredients that would be needed to create it.

Review

- As a class, have pupils discuss each step in order.

Comprehension

Teacher Information

- See the 'Teacher Information' in the 'Text' section opposite.

Introduction

- Pupils take it in turns to retell how they would make porridge. The correct sequence of the steps is very important in a recipe.

Development

- Discuss the comprehension activities on page 98, then allow the pupils to complete the page independently.

- Questions 5, 6 and 7 will have very different answers, so this can lead to a discussion.

Differentiated Individual/Paired/Group Work

- Have pupils work in pairs to write a recipe for their favourite meal. Encourage them to follow the recipe layout and to use the porridge recipe as a template (stating how many it will serve, the list of ingredients and the steps).

- With adult support, have groups work to create porridge according to the recipe. They must be encouraged to read out each step clearly and follow the instructions. Discuss issues such as hygiene and safe food preparation. (Alternatively, do this as a whole class activity and ask groups to perform different steps in the recipe.)

Review

- Have pupils read out their recipe for their favourite meal.

Word Reading

Teacher Information

- The activities on page 99 focus on words that end in 'nk', syllables, words with 'oa' like 'oats' and words with 'ew' like 'flew'.

Introduction

- Reread the text, but first explain to the pupils that the focus will be on words. While reading, ask the pupils to underline the word 'simmer' (it occurs twice in the recipe).

Development

- Ask pupils to find the word 'sprinkle' in the text. Focus their attention on the 'nk'. Use their phonic knowledge to use the vowels before the 'nk': -ank, -ink, -onk, -unk. Ask pupils to think of words that could be made with these endings.

- Revise syllables. Discuss words that have more than two syllables. Talk about rules that might help pupils decide where the syllables are. Have pupils clap out syllables in words they have met previously.

- Introduce words with 'oa'. Use the word 'oat(s)' which appears in the recipe. Discuss how to read this word. Underline the 'oa' and discuss how it sounds. Use a sentence such as 'I left my coat on the boat and it got soaked.' Underline the 'oa' and ensure that pupils can read the sentence accurately.

- Question 7 focuses on words with 'ew' like in the word 'flew'. Use a sentence with both 'oa' and 'ew' to focus on both sounds. Use the sentence 'The new coach had to chew his stew.'

- Discuss the word reading activities on page 99, then allow the pupils to complete the page independently.

Differentiated Individual/Paired/Group Work

- Have pupils think of other 'nk' words that they could write into the grid in question 2. These words could be based on the words they orally discussed earlier in the lesson.

- Challenge highly confident readers to write the words in question 4 in sentences. Ask them to try and include two words in the same sentence.

Review

- As a class, compare pupils' lists containing 'nk' words. In addition, ask some volunteers to read out their sentences of words with 'oa'.

Assessment

C13	Ask each pupil to orally explain the steps involved in making porridge.
	When listening to this account, note how well they explain the steps and if they sequence the steps correctly.
WR3	Present the following list of words to each pupil. Ask the pupil to read each word. Note how well they apply phonic knowledge and blend sounds.
	flew, thank, road, blew, soak, drink, coach, toast, drew, chunk

Answers

Comprehension

1. title, steps or instructions, list of ingredients and equipment, the name of the thing you are making
2. pinhead or steel-cut oatmeal
3. a long wooden stick for stirring
4. So the pot does not get too hot and porridge does not stick to the bottom; i.e. heat is distributed more evenly across the bottom of the pot.
5. Answers will vary.
6. The porridge would stick to the pot and form lumps.
7. Answers will vary.

Word Reading

1. bank, sink, think, chunk
2. -ank = bank; -ink = sink, think; -unk = chunk
3. (a) 3   (b) 2   (c) 2
4. soak, toast, oak, boat, road, coach, coat, goal
5. (a) road   (b) goal   (c) coach   (d) boat
6. oak and soak, coat and boat
7. stew, new, grew, flew

How to Make Porridge – 1

Read the recipe.

Follow the instructions to make porridge.

You will need:

- 100 grams pinhead (steel-cut) oatmeal
- 850 mL water or milk (or a mixture of water and milk)
- good pinch salt
- spurtle or wooden spoon for stirring
- pot with a heavy bottom and a lid
- cold milk or cream for serving
- bowl and spoon

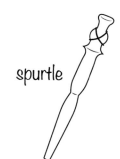

spurtle

Steps:

1. Place water in pot and bring to boil.
2. Turn heat down and sprinkle oats on top. Stir.
3. Bring back to boil, stirring all the time.
4. Turn heat down, cover with lid and simmer for 10 minutes.
5. Add salt and simmer for another 10–15 minutes.
6. Stir every few minutes so porridge does not stick to pot and there are no lumps.
7. Pour into bowl. (Sprinkle on more salt if you like, then add milk or cream.)
8. Eat and enjoy!

How did you do?

Do you think you could make porridge? Do you think it will taste yummy?

My learning log	When I read this recipe, I could read:	☐ all of it. ☐ most of it. ☐ parts of it.

How to Make Porridge – 2

1. Tick the parts of a recipe.

   title ☐   steps or instructions ☐   Once upon a time ☐

   list of ingredients and equipment ☐   rhyming words ☐

   the name of the thing you are making ☐

   And they lived happily ever after ☐

2. What special oatmeal must be used to make porridge?

   _____

3. What is a spurtle? _____

   _____

4. Why does the pot need a heavy bottom?

   _____

   _____

5. What other food or drink can be served with cream?

   _____

6. What would happen if you did not keep on stirring the porridge while it was cooking?

   _____

   _____

7. Have you made or eaten porridge? ☐ Yes ☐ No
   Write about what it tasted and looked like.

   _____

   _____

My learning log	While doing these activities:		
	I found Q _____ easy.	I found Q _____ tricky.	I found Q _____ fun.

How to Make Porridge – 3

1. Write words with the 'n' sound before 'k' like 'spri**nk**le.

    ba_____   si_____   thi_____   chu_____

2. Use the words in question 1 to complete these '-nk' boxes.

-ank	-ink	-unk

3. How many syllables in:

    (a) instructions? ☐   (b) oatmeal? ☐   (c) wooden? ☐

4. Write and read words with 'oa' like 'oats' and 'oatmeal'.

    s_____k   t_____st   _____k   b_____t

    r_____d   c_____ch   c_____t   g_____l

5. Fill in the missing 'oa' words. Use the words in question 4 to help you.

    (a) There are so many cars on the _____ today.

    (b) The football player scored a brilliant _____.

    (c) The football _____ was delighted with the players.

    (d) The _____ had a lovely sail.

6. There are two pairs of rhyming words in question 4. Write them.

rhyming pair 1	rhyming pair 2

7. Write and read new words with '-ew' like 'few'.

    st_____   n_____   gr_____   fl_____

My learning log	Tick if you can read the following words:
	☐ drink ☐ road ☐ goal ☐ chew ☐ nephew

The Pedlar of Swaffham

Curriculum Links

Activity	Code	Objective	Outcome
Text	C3 C9	• Become very familiar with folk tales, retelling them and considering their particular characteristics • Discuss the significance of the title and events	• Can retell a folk tale • Can explain events in a folk tale
Comprehension	C10 C11 C12	• Make inferences on the basis of what is being said and done • Predict what might happen on the basis of what has been read so far • Participate in discussion about what is read to them, taking turns and listening to what others say	• Can use a text to make inferences • Can predict the actions of characters • Can discuss a folk tale with others
Word Reading	WR2 WR5	• Respond speedily with the correct sound to graphemes • Read words containing taught GPCs and -ed and -tch endings	• Can read words with 'ea' like 'dream' • Can read words with '-ed' and '-tch' in them

Additional Teacher Information

Definition of Terms

Text
A book or other written or printed work, regarded in terms of its content rather than its physical form.

Folk tale
A folk tale is a story passed from one generation to the next by word of mouth rather than being written down. A folk tale may include sayings, superstitions, social rituals, and legends or lore about the weather, animals or plants.

Links to other Curriculum Areas

• Geography – Locational knowledge (the town of Swaffham, Norfolk); Human and physical geography (basic geographical vocabulary including bridge and town)

Terminology for Pupils

folk tale
word
fairy tale
text
verb

Suggested Reading

• *The Pedlar of Swaffham* by Kevin Crossley-Holland
• *Caps for Sale* by Esphyr Slobodkina
• *Perkin the Pedlar* by Eleanor Farjeon

Text

Teacher Information

- The pedlar is thought to be a man named John Chapman whose name appears in a list of church benefactors from the 15th century. In Swaffham, there are images of the pedlar and his dog in glass windows of the church and in pubs. Many carved statues are found throughout the church.
- Teachers may wish to help pupils find the location of Swaffham, Norfolk, on a map.

Introduction

- Ask the pupils if they have heard of the folk tale 'The Pedlar of Swaffham'. Discuss what a pedlar is. Tell the pupils that they are going to read a folk tale. Discuss with the class if they know some of the features of a folk tale.

Development

- Read and discuss the text with the pupils. Assist them with any unfamiliar words such as 'pedlar', 'goods', 'decided', 'laughed', 'Swaffham' and 'Norfolk'. Question pupils to gauge their understanding of what they have listened to or read.
- While reading, observe to see how pupils use phonic skills and knowledge to decode words. Assist pupils to decode more difficult words.
- If reading the text together as a class, correct inaccurate reading.

Differentiated Individual/Paired/Group Work

- In pairs, ask pupils to orally summarise the folk tale to each other. Partner A must listen while partner B retells the story and only correct or add in details at the end. Partner A then retells the story.
- In groups have pupils prepare the text for a dramatisation. Each group will need a few narrators, the pedlar and the shopkeeper. Allow each group sufficient time to go through the text and decide which parts of the text to read. Teacher help will be required with some groups.

Review

- Allow each group to perform their dramatisation for the rest of the class.

Comprehension

Teacher Information

- See the 'Teacher Information' in the 'Text' section.

Introduction

- Have pupils take it in turns to retell the folk tale in their own words, sequencing the events correctly.

Development

- Discuss the comprehension activities on page 104, then allow pupils to complete the page independently.
- Compare their answers to questions 8, 9 and 10, as these will have varied answers.

Differentiated Individual/Paired/Group Work

- Ask the pupils to write a short paragraph about what they would do if they found a pot of gold coins. Less able readers could write a few sentences on this topic.
- Ask pupils to work in pairs and draw one of the pictures they think they might see of the pedlar if they went to Swaffham.

Review

- As a class, ask pupils to read out their paragraph telling what they would do if they found a pot of gold coins.

Word Reading

Teacher Information

- The activities on page 105 focus on words with 'tch' like 'catch', words with '-ed' at the end and words with 'ea' like 'dream'.

Introduction

- Reread the text, but first explain to the pupils that the focus will be on words. While reading, ask the pupils to underline any words that are based on the word dream: dream, dreams, dreamt.

Development

- Questions 1 and 2 examine the 'tch' ending of words.
- Questions 2 and 3 ask pupils to look at the '-ed' endings of words.
- Introduce the pupils to words with 'ea', such as 'dream'. Write the sentence 'I dreamt a dream about a mean seal.' on the board. Underline the 'ea' in the words. Read the sentence emphasising the 'ea' sound. Ensure pupils can read the words. Questions 4 and 5 give considerable practice to pupils with such words.

Differentiated Individual/Paired/Group Work

- Have pupils use the words in question 4 to make their own sentences. Can they use two words in the same sentence?
- Ask the pupils to work in pairs and to discuss the shopkeeper and pedlar. They could write down ways they were the same and ways they were different. Encourage them to use information from the folk tale to help them.

Review

- Ask the class to read out some of their sentences with 'ea' words. Were some pupils able to use two words in the same sentence? Invite a few pupils to share their sentences with two or more words in the same sentence.

	Assessment
C3	Ask pupils to work in pairs. Ask them to take turns retelling the folk tale. As the teacher listens to the two pupils, note how well each pupil recalled the events in the story. Also note how well the pupils listened to one another and if they repeated what had already been said.
WR5	Ask pupils to add '-ed' to the following words, if they can take '-ed'. Ask pupils to read out the words as they complete them: catch, clean, clear, fetch, watch, hear, each, witch, leaf, match

Answers

Comprehension

1. Long ago
2. … lived happily ever after.
3. He had the same dream about hearing good news at London Bridge three nights in a row.
4. a person who travels to different towns selling goods
5. Answers will vary.
6. orchard
7. Answers will vary.
8. Answers may include: He went back to work and kept being a shopkeeper for the rest of his life.
9. Answers may include: He worked hard and was a good man.
10. Yes—He used his riches to fix the church.

Word Reading

1. watched
2. –ed
3. (a) walked, reached, laughed, called
   (b) walk, reach, laugh, call
4. each, near, sea, seal, beard, cream, clean, mean, meat, hear, leaf, clear
5. sea, seal, meal, mean, meat, neat, near, clear.
   New word is clear.

The Pedlar of Swaffham – 1

Read the folk tale.

Long ago in the town of Swaffham, in Norfolk, there lived a pedlar. He was very poor but he worked very hard. He walked around towns, with his pack on his back and his dog at his heels, selling goods.

One night, the pedlar dreamt that if he went to London Bridge, he would hear good news. He dreamt the same dream three nights in a row so he decided to go to London.

It was a long way. The pedlar and his dog finally reached London Bridge. For two days, the pedlar stood on the bridge. There were many shops nearby. On the third day, a shopkeeper spoke to him.

'What are you doing here?' he asked. 'I have watched you. You have not sold any goods or begged for money.'

The pedlar replied, 'I have nothing to sell and no wish to beg for money. I have come a long way.' The pedlar told the shopkeeper about his dreams.

The shopkeeper laughed. 'You are a fool to make such a long trip. For two nights, I dreamt I was in a town called Swaffham in an orchard behind a pedlar's house. I dreamt that if I dug behind a great oak tree, I would find a pot of gold coins. I am too wise to make a long trip because of a dream. Go home and work.'

The pedlar was very happy. He did not say a word to the shopkeeper. He went quickly back home. In the orchard behind his house, he dug a hole behind the great oak tree. He found a pot of gold coins.

The pedlar was very rich. He was a good man so he used his riches to fix the church. He lived happily ever after.

Today, a sign in the town of Swaffham shows the pedlar and his dog. There are many pictures around the town of the pedlar who followed his dreams.

My learning log	When I read this folk tale, I could read:	☐ all of it. ☐ most of it. ☐ parts of it.

The Pedlar of Swaffham – 2

1. Which two words begin this folk tale? _____

2. Which words usually end a folk tale or fairy tale?

   _____

3. What event made the pedlar decide to go to London Bridge?

   _____

4. What is a pedlar? _____

   _____

5. Tick the places you have heard of or visited.

   Swaffham ☐   Norfolk ☐   London Bridge ☐

6. Which word means 'a piece of land planted with

   fruit trees'? _____

7. Tick the words that you already knew the meaning of before reading the text.

   town ☐   poor ☐   news ☐   goods ☐

        trip ☐   dream ☐   coin ☐

8. What do you think happened to the shopkeeper?

   _____

9. Why do you think the pedlar was rewarded with a pot of gold coins?

   _____

10. Do you think the pedlar was grateful for his riches? [Yes] [No]

   Why? _____

My learning log	While doing these activities:		
	I found Q _____ easy.	I found Q _____ tricky.	I found Q _____ fun.

The Pedlar of Swaffham – 3

1. Which word in the text has 'tch' like 'catch' and 'fetch'?

_____

2. What ending has been added to 'watched' to make

a new verb from 'watch'? _____

3. (a) Circle other verbs with '-ed' on the end.

walked	reached	laughed	called	stood

(b) Write each word without the ending '-ed'.

_____

4. Write and read words with 'ea' like 'dream'.

_____ch   n_____r   s_____   s_____l

b_____rd   cr_____m   cl_____n   m_____n

m_____t   h_____r   l_____f   cl_____r

5. Follow these instructions in order.

1. Start with 'sea'.	
2. Add an 'l' to the end.	
3. Change 's' to 'm'.	
4. Change 'l' to 'n'.	
5. Change 'n' to 't'.	
6. Change 'm' to 'n'.	
7. Change 't' to 'r'.	
8. Change 'n' to 'cl'.	
The new word is:	

My learning log	Colour:	I can read words with 'tch' at the end.	yes / no
		I can read words like *clean*, *clear* and *beard*.	yes / no

Curriculum Links

Activity	Code	Objective	Outcome
Text	C3	• Become familiar with traditional tales and consider their particular characteristics	• Can discuss the characteristics of a folk tale
	C4	• Recognise and join in with predictable phrases	• Can repeat predictable phrases
	C9	• Discuss the significance of the title and events	• Can discuss the events in a folk tale
Comprehension	C10	• Make inferences on the basis of what is being said and done	• Can use the information to infer meaning
	C11	• Predict what might happen on the basis of what has been read so far	• Can predict based on the details in a text
	C13	• Explain clearly their understanding of what is read to them	• Can answer questions about the folk tale
Word Reading	WR1	• Apply phonic knowledge and skills as the route to decode words	• Can use syllables
	WR2	• Respond speedily with the correct sound to graphemes	• Can read words with '-y' like 'family'
			• Can read words with 'ee', 'ea' and 'air'

Additional Teacher Information

Definition of Terms

Title
The name of a book, composition or other artistic work.

Text
A book or other written or printed work, regarded in terms of its content rather than its physical form.

Folk tale
A folk tale is a story passed from one generation to the next by word of mouth rather than being written down. A folk tale may include sayings, superstitions, social rituals, and legends or lore about the weather, animals or plants.

Story
An account of imaginary or real people and events told for entertainment.

Links to other Curriculum Areas

• Science – Animals, including humans (Identify and name the basic parts of the human body)

Terminology for Pupils

folk tale
word
story
title
sentence
syllable
text
sound

Suggested Reading

• *The Lonely Little Scary* by Albert Jamae [Kindle Edition]
• *Little Ghost and Glowing Heart* by ReGina L. Norlinde [Kindle Edition]
• *In a Dark, Dark Wood* by Jessica Souhami
• *A Dark, Dark Tale* by Ruth Brown

Text

Teacher Information

- This Scottish folk tale has been shortened for ease of reading for young children. A complete version may be found at <http://www.authorama.com/english-fairy-tales-35.html>.

- Young children enjoy simple scary stories. The repetitive words and phrases make the stories fun and easy to read, and help develop fluency and confidence. Read a number of times to add expression.

Introduction

- Discuss folk tales the class may have read previously. Ask them to identify the features that they think are typical of folk tales. Explain that today they are going to read a folk tale called 'The Strange Visitor'. Ask them, based on the title, to predict what they think the folk tale will be about. If time permits, make a list of the suggestions and compare these after reading the story.

Development

- Read and discuss the text with the pupils. Assist them with any unfamiliar words such as 'strange', 'company', 'thighs' and 'knowledge'. Question pupils to gauge their understanding of what they have listened to or read. Ask them why they think the woman was spinning. Why did she want company?

- While reading, observe to see how pupils use phonic skills and knowledge to decode words. Assist pupils to decode more difficult words. If reading the text together as a class, correct inaccurate reading.

Differentiated Individual/Paired/Group Work

- Ask pupils to create a picture showing what they think the visitor looks like. More able readers could draw a series of pictures (in the order of the folk tale) showing the 'growth' of the visitor.

- In pairs, the pupils can be asked to predict what happened next. Once they have decided, they can write a few sentences explaining what they think happens.

Review

- As a class, discuss some of the predictions that pupils have made. Look for similarities and differences among the predictions. Discuss how in folk tales, the ending is often left to the reader's imagination.

Comprehension

Teacher Information

- See the 'Teacher Information' section in the 'Text' column.

Introduction

- Pupils take it in turns to retell the folk tale. Can they remember the correct sequence of the parts of the body?

Development

- Discuss the comprehension activities on page 110, then allow the pupils to complete the page independently.

- Compare their answers to questions 5, 6 and 8, which should generate a lot of discussion.

Differentiated Individual/Paired/Group Work

- In groups, have the pupils rehearse ways to read/tell the folk tale. Encourage them to think about ways that the folk tale could be said/read to heighten the scare factor. The pupils can decide to add dramatisation to their retelling.

Review

- Ask each group to retell or read the folk tale. Have a class vote to see which group did the most convincing job.

Word Reading

Teacher Information

- The activities on page 111 focus on syllables, a range of sounds in words, words that end in '-y' like 'company' and vocabulary to do with the body.

Introduction

- Reread the text, but first explain to the pupils that the focus will be on words. While reading, ask the pupils to underline all the different parts of the body that are mentioned in the text.

Development

- Revise work already completed on syllables. Use words already learned and see if pupils can divide the word into syllables. Play a game where the teacher says some words divided into syllables: some correctly divided and others incorrectly divided. Pupils must identify which words were correctly divided.

- Question 2 presents a number of sounds found in the story. Have pupils sound these out and think of words that contain these sounds.

- Present words ending in –y with the /i:/ sound such as very, happy, funny, party and family. Ensure pupils hear the /i:/ sound. Explain that when they hear this sound at the end of words, the letter to use is 'y'. Questions 3 and 4 provide practice with this sound. Ensure that the pupils can read each word.

- Question 5 asks pupils to read words based on parts of the body. Ensure pupils can read these words. Talk about the silent 'k' in 'knee'.

- Discuss the word reading activities on page 111, then allow pupils to complete the page independently.

Differentiated Individual/Paired/Group Work

- In pairs, ask pupils to draw the outline of a human body and label the different parts of the body using the words they have met in this unit. They should be careful with the spelling of the words.

- Pupils can be asked to write the words in question 3 in sentences of their own. More able readers can try and write sentences that contain more than one of the words.

Review

- As a class, clap out the syllables to the following words: hospital, basketball, calendar, computer, jump, paper, pencil and pen.

Assessment

C4	Ask the pupils to compose a short story based on 'The Strange Visitor' using some predictable phrases. They will need a story template, so the following could be used: One day, I was playing in the garden, wishing for company. In came a _____. They/It sat down on the _____. I kept playing and wishing for company.
WR1	Ask pupils to listen to the following words and then decide how to spell them. They will be using knowledge of syllables and the /i:/ sound: very, angry, happy, sunny, company After they have written the words down, have them check by using lines to divide the words into syllables.

Answers

Comprehension

1. spinning wheel
2. (a) a friend or other people
3. Yes—Answers will vary.
4. 'In came ...',
 '... sat down on ...',
 'The woman kept spinning and wishing for company.'
5. No—Answers will vary.
6. Answers will vary.
7. All body parts should be ticked.
8. Answers will vary.

Word Reading

1. (a) com/pan/y   (b) spin/ning   (c) wish/ing
2. (a) meet   (b) bread   (c) train   (d) chair
 (e) right   (f) start   (g) made   (h) brown
3. happy, family, funny, party, very, sunny, many, nearly
4. (a) family   (b) sunny   (c) party, funny
5. X = chest, knee, nose, lip

The Strange Visitor – 1

Read the folk tale.

One night, a woman sat at her spinning wheel and wished for company.

In came a pair of feet. The woman kept spinning and wishing for company.

In came a pair of legs. They sat down on the feet. The woman kept spinning and wishing for company.

In came a pair of thighs. They sat down on the legs. The woman kept spinning and wishing for company.

In came a pair of hips. They sat down on the thighs. The woman kept spinning and wishing for company.

In came a waist. It sat down on the hips. The woman kept spinning and wishing for company.

In came a pair of shoulders. They sat down on the waist. The woman kept spinning and wishing for company.

In came a pair of arms. They sat down on the shoulders. The woman kept spinning and wishing for company.

In came a pair of hands. They sat down on the arms. The woman kept spinning and wishing for company.

In came a neck. It sat down on the hands. The woman kept spinning and wishing for company.

In came a big head. It sat down on the neck.

'How did you get such a big head?' asked the woman.

'Much knowledge!' said the visitor.

'What are you here for?' asked the woman.

'YOU!' yelled the visitor.

My learning log	When I read this folk tale, I could read:	☐ all of it. ☐ most of it. ☐ parts of it.

The Strange Visitor – 2

1. Which two words mean 'a machine for spinning yarn with a spindle and a wheel'?

   _____

2. The word 'company' in the story means:

   (a) a friend or other people ☐   (b) a business ☐

3. Does the title tell what the story is about? Yes No Why?

   _____

4. Write words or a sentence used over and over again in the folk tale.

   _____

   _____

5. Do you think the woman was glad she wished for company?

   Yes No Why?

   _____

   _____

6. What do you think the strange visitor will do to the woman?

   _____

   _____

7. Tick the body parts that you have like the strange visitor.

   feet ☐   legs ☐   thighs ☐   hips ☐   waist ☐

   shoulders ☐   arms ☐   hands ☐   neck ☐   head ☐

8. Write the name of another scary story you have heard or read.

   _____

My learning log	While doing these activities:		
	I found Q _____ easy.	I found Q _____ tricky.	I found Q _____ fun.

The Strange Visitor – 3

1. Write the words correctly in the syllable boxes.

(a) company

(b) spinning

(c) wishing

2. Make a new word like each one from the text. The sound made by the letters in bold must be the same in both words.

(a) f**ee**t   m_____t

(b) h**ea**d   br_____d

(c) w**ai**st   tr_____n

(d) p**ai**r   ch_____

(e) th**igh**   r_____t

(f) **ar**ms   st_____t

(g) cam**e**   m____d_____

(h) d**ow**n   br_____n

3. Add '-y' like in 'company' to finish these words. Read each word.

happ_____   famil_____   funn_____   part_____

ver_____   sunn_____   man_____   nearl_____

4. Use the words in question 3 to help you complete the sentences.

(a) My whole _____ are going on holiday together.

(b) The weather today is very _____.

(c) The clown was at the _____ and he was

_____.

5. Here are some parts of the body. Tick if the word is mentioned in the story. Put an X if it isn't.

hip ☐   chest ☐   knee ☐   shoulder ☐

nose ☐   lip ☐   neck ☐   leg ☐

My learning log	*Colour:*	I can say the syllables in different words.	yes / no
		I can read words like *family*, *party* and *nearly*.	yes / no

The Field of Weeds

Curriculum Links

Activity	Code	Objective	Outcome
Text	C3 C6	• Become very familiar with traditional tales, retelling them and considering their particular characteristics • Discuss word meanings, linking new meanings to those already known	• Can retell a folk tale • Can explain words like 'harvest', 'leprechaun' and 'garter'
Comprehension	C9 C12	• Discuss the significance of the title and events • Participate in discussion about what is read to them, taking turns and listening to what others say	• Can discuss the folk tale with others
Word Reading	WR1 WR3	• Apply phonic knowledge and skills as the route to decode words • Read accurately by blending sounds in unfamiliar words containing GPCs that have been taught	• Can read and understand some homophones • Can read words with 'aw' like 'saw' • Can read words with 'ie' like 'field'

Additional Teacher Information

Definition of Terms

Title
The name of a book, composition or other artistic work.

Folk tale
A folk tale is a story passed from one generation to the next by word of mouth rather than being written down. A folk tale may include sayings, superstitions, social rituals, and legends or lore about the weather, animals or plants.

Story
An account of imaginary or real people and events told for entertainment.

Character
A person in a novel, play or film.

Links to other Curriculum Areas

• Science – Plants (Identify and name a variety of common wild and garden plants)

Terminology for Pupils

folk tale
title
event
beginning
ending
character
word
story
sound
homophone

Suggested Reading

• *Clever Tom and the Leprechaun: An Old Irish Story* by Linda Shute
• *Tim O'Toole and the Wee Folk* by Gerald McDermott
• *That's What Leprechauns Do* by Eve Bunting
• *The Leprechaun's Gold* by Pamela Duncan Edwards

Text

Teacher Information

- Leprechauns are part of Irish legend. They are supposed to have a pot of gold and, if caught, they will reveal where the pot of gold is.

Introduction

- Ask the pupils if they have ever heard of leprechauns. Ask them to describe what they think they look like. Where did they hear about them? Ask them if they know any legends about leprechauns. Explain that they are going to read a folk tale about a man who found a leprechaun and what happened when he tried to find the pot of gold.

Development

- Read and discuss the text with the pupils. Assist them with any unfamiliar words such as 'rambling', 'noise', 'hedge', 'leprechaun', 'fields', 'pointed', 'decided', 'garter', 'touch', 'spade', 'none' and 'tricked'.

- Question pupils to gauge their understanding of what they have listened to or read.

- While reading, observe to see how pupils use phonic skills and knowledge to decode words. Encourage the pupils to utilise phonic knowledge and skills while reading so that decoding becomes automatic and reading more fluent. Assist pupils to decode more difficult words.

- If reading the text together as a class, correct inaccurate reading.

Differentiated Individual/Paired/Group Work

- After reading, have a whole class discussion. How did the leprechaun trick Tom? Did Tom do the right thing? What could Tom have done differently? During the discussion, encourage pupils to employ courteous listening skills such as turn-taking and listening to the points of views of others.

- In pairs, have pupils discuss what they would have done if they were in Tom's place. How would they have made the leprechaun give them the pot of gold?

Review

- As a class, invite volunteers to come and tell what they would have done in Tom's place. Finish the lesson by reviewing some of the words encountered in the story. Can the pupils read and explain these words?

Comprehension

Teacher Information

- See the 'Teacher Information' in the 'Text' section.
- There are a number of texts that could be read aloud for pupils. These can be found in the 'Suggested Reading' section.

Introduction

- Pupils take it in turns to retell the folk tale in their own words, sequencing the events correctly.

Development

- Discuss the comprehension activities on page 116, then allow pupils to complete the page independently.
- Compare their answers to questions 2, 4 and 7, as these will have varied answers.

Differentiated Individual/Paired/Group Work

- Ask highly confident readers to summarise the story in a few paragraphs. Less able readers could summarise the story in a few sentences.

Review

- As a class, have pupils revise the story and discuss any parts of it that they thought were interesting.

Word Reading

Teacher Information

- The activities on page 117 focus on words with 'aw' like 'saw', words with 'ie' like 'field' and homophones.

Introduction

- Reread the text, but first explain to the pupils that the focus will be on words. While reading, ask the pupils to underline any plural words they find in the text.

Development

- Introduce the pupils to words with 'aw', such as 'saw'. Write the sentence 'The hawk saw a straw on the lawn.' on the board. Underline the 'aw' in the words. Read the sentence emphasising the 'aw' sound. Ensure pupils can read the words.

- Use a similar approach with words with 'ie' in the words such as 'field'. Write a sentence such as 'The chief went for a brief walk in the field.' Underline the 'ie' in the words and read the sentence emphasising these parts.

- The homophones introduced here are 'where/wear', 'bear/bare', 'sun/son', 'ant/aunt', 'hair/hare' and 'sea/see'. These are common homophones that Year 1 pupils can master. Explain to pupils that these words sound the same but are spelt differently. Explain that it is the meaning of the word which helps us to choose which word to use. Ask the pupils to use the words in oral sentences. To ensure that they know the correct meaning for each word, write the words on flashcards or small posters and point to each one when asking pupils to make up an oral sentence.

- Pupils compete the word reading activities on page 117 independently.

Differentiated Individual/Paired/Group Work

- Have pupils use the words in question 1 to make their own sentences.

- In pairs, have pupils make posters to show the difference between the pairs of homophones. Pictures and a simple sentence should help them show the difference.

Review

- As a class, review the work that was done and have pupils read out their sentences and display their posters. Revise the homophones met in this lesson one more time.

Assessment

C3	Ask pupils to retell the folk tale in their own words, following the correct sequence.
WR1	Have pupils underline the correct word in the sentences below: My (ant/aunt) is my dad's sister. The (hare/hair) ran away from the fox. I can't wait to (sea/see) the (sea/see). The (sun/son) is shining in the sky. The (bear/bare) scared the hawk.
WR3	Present the following list of words to pupils and see if they can read them correctly: piece, crawl, hawk, field, yawn, movie, chief, draw, crawling, thief

Answers

Comprehension

1. All boxes should be ticked.
2. where the events take place
3. (a) weed—a wild and unwanted plant
   (b) garter—a band used to keep socks up
   (c) leprechaun—a small, naughty sprite
   (d) spade—a tool for digging
4. No—because he was tricked once.
5. silly, easily tricked
6. at the end of the rainbow
7. Answers will vary.
8. Answers may vary.

Word Reading

1. (a) yawn   (b) draw   (c) crawl
   (d) paw   (e) jaw   (f) raw
2. (a) crawl   (b) raw   (c) yawn   (d) paw
3. chief, thief
4. (a) piece   (b) believe   (c) grief   (d) movie
5. They sound the same but are written/spelt differently.
6. son – someone's boy, sun – shines in the sky;
   ant – an insect, aunt – parent's sister;
   hair – grows on my head, hare – an animal like a rabbit;
   sea – water in a huge space, see – what my eyes do

The Field of Weeds – 1

Read the folk tale.

One day at harvest time, Tom Fitzpatrick was rambling over the land.

Suddenly, he heard a noise behind a hedge. Tom peeked over the top and saw a leprechaun. He knew if you catch a leprechaun and hold onto him, he must tell you where to find his pot of gold.

Tom quickly grabbed the leprechaun. Tom looked so mean that the leprechaun said he would show him where to find his pot of gold. They set off over the fields. Tom watched the leprechaun all the time. He did not want him to get away.

Soon they came to a great field of weeds. The leprechaun pointed to a large weed.

'If you dig under that weed, you will find a pot of gold', said the leprechaun.

Tom had nothing to dig with. He decided to run home to get a spade. He took the red garter from around one sock. He tied it around the weed. Now he would know where to find the place when he got back.

'Swear you will leave the garter on the weed', he said to the leprechaun. The leprechaun said he would not touch it.

'Can I leave now?' asked the leprechaun.

'I do not need you now', said Tom. So the leprechaun quickly left.

Tom ran home as fast as he could. He got the spade and ran back to the field of weeds. When he got there, he found that none of the weeds had a red garter tied to them.

Tom carried the spade home but no pot of gold. He never forgot how the leprechaun had tricked him.

My learning log	When I read this folk tale, I could read:	☐ all of it. ☐ most of it. ☐ parts of it.

The Field of Weeds – 2

1. Tick the things in the folk tale.

   title ☐   events ☐   a beginning ☐   an ending ☐

   characters ☐   a place where the story happens ☐

2. What does the title tell you?

   _____

3. Match each word to its meaning.

   (a) weed   •   •   a band used to keep socks up

   (b) garter   •   •   a wild and unwanted plant

   (c) leprechaun   •   •   a tool for digging

   (d) spade   •   •   a small, naughty sprite

4. Do you think Tom will trust a leprechaun again?   Yes   No

   Why? _____

5. Tick the words that best describe Tom.

   silly ☐   easily tricked ☐   brave ☐   clever ☐

6. Where do leprechauns usually hide their pot of gold?

   _____

7. Write the name of another story with a leprechaun character or a person named Tom.

   _____

8. Do you think the leprechaun hid his gold in the field of weeds at all?   Yes   No

	While doing these activities:		
ning log	I found Q _____ easy.	I found Q _____ tricky.	I found Q _____ fun.

The Field of Weeds – 3

1. Write and read new words with 'aw' like 'saw'.

    (a) y_____n

    (b) dr_____

    (c) cr_____l

    (d) p_____

    (e) j_____

    (f) r_____

2. Fill in the missing 'aw' words into the blank spaces.

    (a) A baby likes to _____ around the floor.

    (b) It is unsafe to eat _____ chicken.

    (c) I was tired and I started to _____.

    (d) The dog injured his _____.

3. Circle the words with the same sound in the middle as 'field'.

chief	thief	cried	tried	dried

4. Write and read new words with 'ie' like 'field'.

    (a) p_____ce   (b) bel_____ve   (c) gr_____f   (d) mov_____

5. What is special about these pairs of words?

    (a) where *and* wear   (b) bear *and* bare

    _____

6. Here are some more words that sound the same but are spelt
    differently. Read the clues. Colour each clue and the matching word in
    the same colour.

sun	son	ant	aunt
someone's boy	shines in the sky	parent's sister	an insect
hair	**hare**	**sea**	**see**
an animal like a rabbit	grows on my head	what my eyes do	water in a huge space

My learning log	***Colour:***	I can read these words: *raw, crawl, piece* and *field*.	yes / no
		I know the difference between *ant* and *aunt*.	yes / no
		I know the difference between *see* and *sea*.	yes / no

The Beast Inside the Window

Read the recount.

The night was dark and quiet. Mum was cleaning up the kitchen. Dinner was over for another night.

Mum opened the window. The cool breeze came in. The cooking smells went out.

Mum heard the children getting ready for bed. She heard Dad clicking on his computer.

Mum put away the dishes. She wiped the table. She wiped the sink. She wiped the hob. She wiped the oven door.

She hung up the tea towel. She hung up her apron. She made the food jars straight. Everything was clean and tidy.

She started to close the kitchen window. As she pulled it, a large, brown, ugly beast dropped down. It crawled up the window. It looked at Mum with big eyes. The hairs on its legs twitched.

Mum closed the window and pulled down the blind. She trapped the beast between the blind and the window.

'Don't open that blind! There's a beast behind it!' she yelled.

The next day Dad opened the window. A big beetle crawled out and hopped outside. Mum felt better.

I'm glad I don't have to clean up the kitchen!

117

• • • *Reading – Comprehension and Word Reading* • • • • • • • • • • • • • • • • Prim-Ed Publishing • • • • www.prim-ed.com

The Beast Inside the Window

1. What was the large, brown, ugly beast? Tick one.

   ☐ a worm ☐ a snake ☐ a beetle

   `1 mark`

2. Which event happened last? Write L for 'last' next to it.

   (a) Mum opened the kitchen window. _____

   (b) The beetle hopped outside. _____

   (c) The family had dinner. _____

   `1 mark`

3. Why was the kitchen window open? (Two reasons)

   • _____

   • _____

   `2 marks`

4. Why do you think the beetle was on the window?

   _____

   _____

   `1 mark`

5. Why did Mum close the blind and trap the beast? Tick one.

   ☐ She did not want the beast to get into the kitchen.

   ☐ She wanted to keep it and look at it.

   ☐ She wanted the beast to have a nice place to live.

   `1 mark`

Total for this page /6

Name: _____ Class: _____ Date: _____

The Beast Inside the Window

1. Tick two words that have the 'tch' sound.

☐ screen

☐ kitchen

☐ crawled

☐ twitched

1 mark

2. (a) Which two words make up the compound word 'everything'?

_____ and _____

(b) Which two words make up the compound word 'outside'?

_____ and _____

1 mark

3. Circle the words that make up the contraction 'I'm'.

1 mark

| I do | I will | I am |

4. Write the suffix at the end of each word.

(a) cleaning _____

(b) started _____

(c) dishes _____

(d) smells _____

(e) yelled _____

1 mark

| Total for this page | /4 | Total for this assessment | /10 |

The Beast Inside the Window

Genre: Recount

Breakdown of question type/content and mark allocation

Comprehension			Word Reading		
Q 1. Finding information	1 mark		Q 1. 'tch' sound	1 mark	
Q 2. Sequencing	1 mark		Q 2. Compound words	1 mark	
Q 3. Finding information	2 marks		Q 3. Contractions	1 mark	
Q 4. Inferring	1 mark		Q 4. Suffixes	1 mark	
Q 5. Inferring	1 mark				
Sub-total			Sub-total		
			Record the pupil's total result for this assessment.		

Assessment – The Beast Inside the Window

Comprehension ....*Page 119*

1. 'a beetle' should be ticked
2. (b) The beetle hopped outside.
3. to let the cool breeze in; to let the cooking smells out
4. Answers will vary. It may have been hiding, looking for food, trying to get inside etc.
5. She did not want the beast to get into the kitchen.

Word Reading ....*Page 120*

1. kitchen, twitched
2. (a) every, thing   (b) out, side
3. I am
4. (a) -ing   (b) -ed   (c) -es   (d) -s   (e) -ed